Louis Weber, C.E.O.
Publications International, Ltd.
7373 North Cicero Avenue
Lincolnwood, Illinois 60646

Manufactured in the U.S.A.

8 7 6 5 4 3 2 1

ISBN 1-56173-538-8

Fellow Camaro Enthusiasts . . .

Camaro owners who'd like to join like-minded enthusiasts to share information and fellowship are served by two major clubs:

International Camaro Club; 2001 Pittston Ave.; Scranton, PA 18505. Phone: (717) 347-5839.

United States Camaro Club; 3946 Indian Ripple Rd.; Dayton, OH 45440. Phone: (513) 426-6494 (Monday through Friday, daytime hours.)

Owners

Special thanks to the owners of the cars featured in this book for their enthusiastic cooperation. They are listed below, along with the page number(s) on which their cars appear.

Rob Embleton 4, 5, 16, 23; **Ernest Giglotti** 17; **Tom Bigelow** 18, 19; **Ramshead Auto Collection, Robert R. Lotito, Robert Francek** 21; **Mike D'Amico** 22; **Charley Lillard** 24, 25, 36, 37; **Steven Knutsen** 25; **Sandy D'Amico** 26; **Jerry Buczkowski** 27; **Nick D'Amico** 28, 29, 34, 35; **Paul McGuire** 30, 31; **Donald R. Crile** 32, 33; **Tony D'Amico** 38, 39; **Barry Waddell** 52, 53; **Stephen F. Collins** 54, 55; **Dr. Mike Cruz** 56; **Debra L. Hogan** 70, 71; **Richard Matzer** 78, 79

Photography

The editors gratefully acknowledge the cooperation of the following people who have supplied photography to help make this book possible. They are listed below, along with the page number(s) of their photos.

Special thanks to Chuck Jordan, Vice President General Motors Design Staff; Floyd Joliet, General Motors Design Staff; Kari St. Antoine, Mark Broderick, Chevrolet Public Relations.

Sam Griffith 4, 5, 16, 23; **Doug Mitchel** 17, 21, 22, 26, 28, 29, 34, 35, 38, 39; **Bud Juneau** 21, 24, 25, 36, 37; **Mike Mueller** 30, 31, 52, 53, 70, 71, 78, 79; **Milton Gene Kieft** 32, 33; **Nicky Wright** 54, 55; **Vince Manocchi** 56, 57; **Mitch Frumkin** 120, 121; **Chevrolet Motor Division** 124, 125; **Hidden Image/Hans G. Lehmann** 125.

CONTENTS

Personality Keeps It Popular

Not many car models endure for a quarter-century, and of those that do, precious few still draw crowds and sell strongly after continuing for more than a decade in a single form. One of these unusually successful cars is Chevrolet's Camaro. Like the related Pontiac Firebird, the Camaro has managed to maintain a considerable share of the allure that first attracted enthusiasts back in 1967. Blending roguish lines with muscle-flexing performance and a traditional "feel," Camaro can tempt both those who remember it well from prior incarnations, and latter-day fans who weren't even born when the Z-28 ordering code first entered the automotive lexicon.

For car enthusiasts and collectors, Chevrolet was ripe for a meteoric rise to "marque of choice" in the 1970s and beyond. Aside from the Corvette, which has been a collector's item since Day One, the growing interest in Chevys of all kinds was a new development. For years the dominant force in the old-car hobby had been Ford Motor Company—chiefly the Ford Models T, A, and V-8; the Continentals; and the Lincoln-Zephyr. Through the Seventies, the 1965-66 Mustang gained a large following. Still, considering all the hot collector's items carrying Chevrolet badges, Ford was not destined to remain the popularity leader for long.

The year when Chevy became known for something other than just reliable transportation isn't hard to pinpoint. It was 1955, when Ed Cole's remarkable 265 V-8 arrived, wrapped in one of the prettiest bodies of the postwar era. That potent engine also found its way into the Corvette, which has remained a performance car ever since. Today there's not a single undesirable Corvette, and the 1955-57 standard Chevrolet has long been a red-hot item on the collector market.

Led by these two benchmark Chevys, enthusiasm for other models blossomed in the Seventies. Early attention focused on the unique Corvair. It went out of production in 1969, which virtually guaranteed a following of sorts for America's rear-engine compact. Toss in its innovative engineering, sprightly per-formance, and good looks, and it's no wonder that the then-radical Corvair has kept a legion of fans to this day.

In the late Seventies, enthusiasts began turning to other Chevy products, notably the potent Super Sport Impalas and Malibus of the mid-Sixties. Interest in vintage models from the 1930s and '40s also continued strong, of course. By the 1980s, however, the center of attention in Chevy circles shifted to a relative latecomer—the fascinating Camaro.

The Camaro's new-found appeal took some by surprise. After all, it was first produced merely as a response to the competition—namely Mustang—not as a brand-new idea. Compared to the Corvair, it was conventional in the extreme; measured against Corvette, it was somewhat less glamorous; compared to the SS 409, it wasn't even memorably quick (with the exception of the Z-28).

What, then, makes the Camaro so sought-after even today? Above all, the answer must be "personality." Every Camaro has had it: the RS (Rally Sport) with its sporty lines and winning perfor-mance; the Z-28 with its competitive prowess; the 1970 second-generation coupe with its peerless styling. And let's not ignore the long-lived third-generation design, which has kept the original ponycar spirit alive since 1982, peaking in the race-based IROC-Z of the late Eighties. Few would doubt that the fourth generation, re-engineered for a 1993 debut, will carry on the mystique with dignity.

Camaro was not designed to be basic transportation, or even to be especially practical. What it was—and continues to be—was a smooth, powerful, personal road machine, intended mainly for those who enjoyed motoring for sheer pleasure. It had looks, speed, handling, comfort—even luxury in some models. Camaro was roomier than an MG, less expensive than a Porsche, more reliable than a Jaguar, and (in some guises) as fast as a Ferrari. And from the first, the Camaro was offered with so many options that you could literally "build" yourself the exact car to fit your personal needs and tastes. Today, you can probably find your ideal among older-model Camaros on the collector market, if you're patient enough.

That the Camaro continues with its original character is especially remarkable in view of what happened in the Seventies. That was the decade that saw oil shortages, dollar-a-gallon gas, and government reg-ulations that changed the shape of the American car—not to mention the demise of most of the Camaro's early competitors. In the safety- and economy-conscious Eighties, the notion of performance-oriented cars faced a further prospect of extinction. Today, except for Ford's indestructible Mustang, all that's left from the ponycar era is this handsome Chevy and its similarly crowd-pleasing Pontiac counterpart, the Firebird.

Part of the Camaro's special magic is that the car has remained faithful to a time-honored theme of sporty, affordable personal transportation. Yet its sheer endurance, its very survival in a changing world, is also an important part of the mystique. Still part of the Chevrolet lineup, and likely to remain so for some time, Camaro continues to win new fans, while Corvair, for example, does not. Camaro lovers now include not only those who bought a new one yesterday, but also those who, in their younger days, might have owned a '67 Rally Sport or a '70 Z-28. They remember what those cars were like, and might now treat themselves to "one like I used to have."

This book is dedicated to Camaro enthusiasts of all ages, and owners of all models. You'll find insight into the car's four design generations: 1967-69, 1970-81, 1982 to the present day, and the newest Camaro, bowing for '93. In these pages are Camaro's past, present, and its promising future—a future which still appears to be secure as the fourth-generation design takes center stage.

So, settle back and enjoy the ride. And as you do, remember the traditional toast of Bugatti enthusiasts, which is no less apt for Camaro: *Viva la marque!*

Twenty-five years. Time enough to grow, to improve and change. Time enough, certainly, to thrill, which is what Camaro has done so well, ever since the stunning first-generation models, typified by the 1967 RS Coupe (*below*). It's been

Chapter One
First Generation: Challenges and Choices

Rivalry between Chevrolet and Ford had been the rule as far back as the 1930s. Development of Chevy's Camaro and Ford's Mustang tightened that competition—a ponycar battle that persists into the Nineties.

Some people believe that if it hadn't been for the Mustang, the Camaro would never have existed. This is something of an oversimplification and misses the real point. By late 1966, when the Camaro was introduced, the demand for such cars already was strong—and still growing. GM was simply responding. Sure, that buyer demand had been generated largely by the Mustang, but the Camaro had actually

started developing long before Ford's ponycar arrived.

Interest in sporty, close-coupled compacts that could seat two comfortably (four in a pinch) reaches back at least to 1956. That was the year Studebaker fielded its first Hawks—nimble, fast road machines, descended from the startling '53 Starlight coupe, which looked different and performed considerably better than the average family sedan. Studebaker even helped set the stage for the subsequent muscle car era by stuffing a big 352-cid Packard V-8 into its Golden Hawk, before turning to supercharged power for '57.

For 1958, Ford punched its pretty two-

seat Thunderbird out to a four-seat configuration, which also introduced a radical new body design that met with overwhelming acceptance. GM replied with the Pontiac Grand Prix in 1962 and the stunning four-place Buick Riviera the following year. Similar concepts followed, such as Oldsmobile's front-wheel-drive Toronado of 1966. The race was on.

Until Mustang, four-seat "personal" cars had been mainly upper-price luxury models. But stylists and engineers at General Motors were thinking about something in the lower-price class a good six years before the Mustang debuted in early 1964. Pontiac designer Bill Porter,

Initially scorned by some as a compromised "committee car" conceived as a response to Mustang, the Camaro quickly established its credentials.

for example, told author Michael Lamm, "As early as 1958, I remember a four-passenger, sporty type car of the general size and weight class of the Mustang being worked on in an advanced studio. In the early '60s, similar cars were developed from time to time. Everyone wanted to do one, but at the time there was really no corporate interest."

The first low-priced "personal" car to score with the public was created almost by accident, when Chevrolet added bucket seats to its Corvair sports coupe late in the 1960 model year. Compared to the more cheaply furnished 500 and 700 versions, the new Corvair Monza 900 was an eye-popper. It offered a color-keyed interior, comfortable vinyl bucket seats, and (in 1961) the option of a four-speed manual gearbox. Monzas sold like hot coffee on a cold morning. Soon they were outselling all other Corvair models combined. Ford and Chrysler, taking due note, rushed to equip their Falcon and Valiant compacts with deluxe interiors, consoles, bucket seats, and floor shifts. This trend ultimately led to the Falcon-based Mustang, whose success is well-known: 100,000 units sold in the first six months, over half a million in the first year.

Mustang's introduction caused no immediate reaction at GM, which took a "wait-and-see" attitude. For a while, GM felt that its forthcoming, fully restyled 1965 Corvair, with a sophisticated four-wheel independent suspension and rear-mounted engine offering up to 180 horsepower, would easily outsell the more pedestrian Mustang. It didn't. By August 1964—only four months after Ford's new "quarter horse" appeared—GM had decided to begin development of a product along comparable lines. Chevy's creation would have a front engine, rear drive, an attractive base price—and would be offered with a large number of extra-cost items so buyers could tailor the car to suit their individual preferences. This last provision was most

Opposite: Early Camaro styling studies, from May and October 1962. Camaro cues are visible here and there, particularly in the nose designs, but these drawings seem more suggestive of luxury tourers than what later became known as ponycars. *Left:* A clay model completed in July 1962, some time before the formal start of project XP-836, carries on the strong luxury feel; resemblance to the '66 Toronado is obvious. Note the intriguing cobra emblem behind the front wheelarch. Aft view is distinguished by tunnelback roof and fender exhaust ports.

This page and opposite: GM's interest in smooth, fluid lines is evident in these 1962-64 styling studies. Note that some of these renderings feature the single bodyside peak that would become a Camaro trademark.

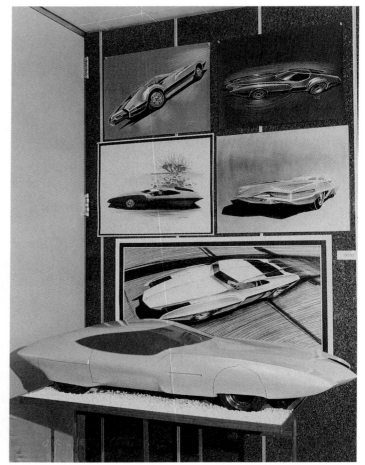

significant. Mustang had demonstrated that a comprehensive options list would allow a basic, inexpensive package to serve as an economy runabout, sporty compact, or a relatively luxurious "personal" car, all at the same time. Despite its many good points, the Corvair never had this kind of versatility. This was one reason why it never outsold the economy Falcon. Another was character. Corvair and its interesting engineering appealed mainly to a fairly small group of knowledgeable enthusiasts, not the much greater number of "mainstream" buyers attracted to the Falcon's anvil-like simplicity.

Early on, it was determined that Chevy's Mustang-fighter would be based on off-the-shelf components shared with a "volume" family model. Product planning and production considerations decreed that the new car should relate closely to the Chevy II, which was set to be completely restyled and re-engineered for 1968. The original Chevy II had also failed to outsell the Falcon, but the 1968 and later models (known simply as Nova from 1969 on) enjoyed much greater success.

The job of shaping what would become the Camaro was handed to the GM Design Center's Chevrolet Studio Two, under Henry E. Haga. The chain of command—important because all echelons had a role in determining Camaro styling—stretched from Haga to David R. Holls, Charles M. Jordan, Irwin W. Rybicki, to design vice president William L. Mitchell.

Mitchell never liked the first-generation Camaro. "It wasn't worth a damn," he remarked to *Car Classics* magazine in 1978. "There were too many people involved." In his view, the styling suffered because the car had to be designed with an eye to sharing components. Dave Holls, then Chevrolet group chief designer, noted two areas where the styling was compromised for just this reason: cowl height and hood length.

The Camaro project was designated "F-car" early on. For general styling inspiration it looked to the Chevrolet Super Nova, a show car first seen at the New York Auto Show in early 1964, shortly before the production Mustang was introduced. The Super Nova was a clean, smooth-lined coupe, but not particularly stunning. It merely expressed GM's mid-Sixties styling philosophy. "Fluidity" is how one staffer explained it: "If you take a heavy wire frame and bend it into the basic 3-dimensional outline of the car you want, then stretch thin canvas over the frame, and if you finally blow compressed air gently into the bottom of the canvas envelope, you get a very natural, free-flowing, unartificial body shape. This fluid form showed up most strikingly in the 1965 crop of General Motors cars."

The emphasis on roundness—ironically, so well expressed in the ill-fated second-generation Corvair—contrasted sharply with the square-rigged lines of contemporary Fords. Seen in profile, the '67 Camaro was smoother, more flowing; that year's Mustang was more angular and abrupt. The two car companies' different approaches are hard to compare objectively. Critics agreed that the Mustang's overall look benefited from its longer hood, while some stylists felt the Camaro, with its shorter hood, looked too much like a Corvair for its own good. Still, the balance of professional judgment is on the side of the Camaro. And significantly, the Mustang's styling became noticeably more

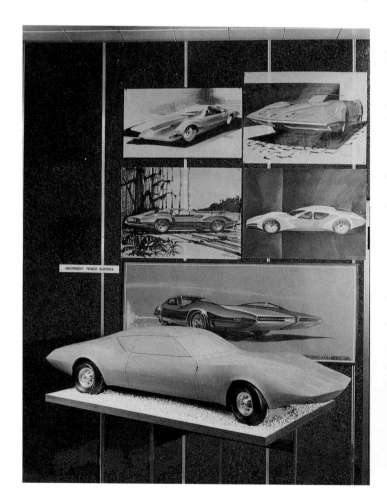

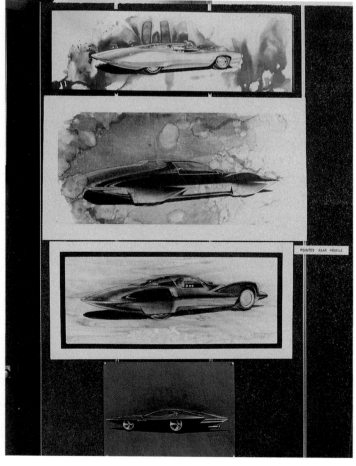

"fluid" in its succeeding design generations.

Henry Haga summarized the GM styling concept as applied to the Camaro: "We felt very strongly about reducing design to its simplest form, using only one peak down each body side, interrupted by accented wheel arches. The profile of the car also was very simple, using the classic approach of crowned fender lines, with their high points directly above the accented wheel arches. We purposefully avoided any contrived design lines and superfluous detail. Even the execution of the wide, horizontal-loop front end and grille, with its hidden headlamps in the Rally Sport variant, was as pure in concept as we could make it."

Interior design was directed by George Angersbach, a specialist in Chevy's smaller cars—Corvette, Corvair, and Nova. Angersbach recalled that the Camaro (and Corvair) borrowed heavily from the dashboard design of the all-new 1968 Corvette, which was being styled at the same time. This layout featured two large round dials set squarely in front of the driver. One problem: the size of the dials left little space ahead of the steering wheel, where sporting drivers might want a bank of auxiliary gauges. A compromise was suggested by interior stylist Sue Vanderbilt, who created a three-dial cluster to mount atop an optional center console. This treatment was continued, using a staggered or "sawtooth" four-dial cluster for 1968 and '69. The console wasn't the best place to put the gauges for easy viewing, but they had to go somewhere.

The Camaro's body was one of the first at GM to be seriously evaluated in a wind tunnel. In those days, GM used the facilities of the Ling-Temco-Vought Aircraft Company in Dallas, Texas. (In 1980, the automaker officially opened its own wind tunnel at the GM Tech Center in Warren, Michigan.) Although the tests were not

Opposite: The familiar lines of the first-generation Camaro are unmistakable on these 1964 clays. Interior mock-up (*third row, left*) shows Corvette influence. Another influence was Mustang, two of which are shown in a July 1964 photo (*bottom*) with a Camaro clay and Chevy's own Corvair Monza. *This page:* Running convertible prototype (*top*) acquired "cocktail shakers" to cure torsional vibration. Panther prototype (*second photo*) lost its name and round taillamps, but the low Camaro stance is apparent. A two-seat roadster (*third photo*) was rejected because of cost; a hatchback sport wagon (*bottom*) was also abandoned.

Although assembled largely from off-the-shelf parts, the Camaro managed a distinct personality—a credit to the committee that created it. The unique front sub-frame was the first application of the idea in a low-priced American car. The rear suspension, however, was something less than state of the art. Camaro shared its cowl with the Chevy II.

conducted until the styling was almost finalized, the Camaro body proved to have excellent aerodynamic characteristics—a tribute to the design team. The only changes necessary were mild modifications to the front fenders and the front pan under the bumper.

One thing the designers didn't get with the first-generation Camaro was a fastback body style. They did create one in mock-up form as a potential answer to the Mustang 2+2. But management insisted on just two models, a coupe and convertible, mostly for cost reasons. Further behind in the running—but still present in the minds and drawings of the designers for a while—were a two-seat cabriolet and a smooth two-door sport-wagon. The consensus is that these extensions were also precluded by cost. GM was, after all, attempting to

match the Mustang's $2500 base price.

A critical engineering decision made right at the outset was to use a front sub-frame in combination with unit construction for the Camaro—and, in due course, the 1968 Nova. This was a fairly unique approach in that the sub-frame was isolated from the body by rubber inserts, or "biscuits," as the engineers called them. This technique had been refined on costlier European unit-body cars, including various Mercedes-Benz models and the larger Opels, but Camaro's was the first application in a low-priced American car. The compromise was highly effective. Unit construction techniques allowed more passenger and luggage space than a body designed for a separate full chassis. The relatively exotic rubber mounts gave a smoother, quieter ride than cars with sub-frames bolted directly to the main bodyshell, like early-Sixties Chrysler products. (In fact, the problem of isolating road noise with a front sub-frame was one of the reasons Imperials of the period stayed with a separate frame.)

The rear suspension was a less happy arrangement. Chevy adopted single-leaf (Mono-Plate) springs used successfully on the Chevy II and Olds Toronado, but this resulted in considerable axle tramp in hard acceleration with the larger V-8 engines. Several quick-fix engineering measures were tried after the first Camaros came off the line. For 1967, the big-engine models were fitted with traction bars, whereas the '68s had staggered shocks. These alterations reduced the axle tramp tendency, but a more sophisticated rear suspension should have been attempted. Again, a tight budget was the limiting factor.

Another early Camaro flaw was rear-end bottoming under heavy loads. This resulted from a decision made during executive reviews of the final prototypes. Originally, the standard Camaro was slated to ride on 13-inch wheels. But these, along with the high cowl, gave the prototypes an ungainly, "small-wheeled" look. To satisfy the sales department, which wanted a more aggressive appearance, engineers lowered the car and substituted 14-inch wheels and tires. The lowering contributed to the bottoming. This problem was never entirely cured on the 1967 models, though rear suspension travel was increased on the '68s to get around it.

One other interesting engineering trick was the use of what GM men called "cocktail shakers"—harmonic shock absorbers located at each corner in Camaro convertibles. Their purpose was to control torsional vibration, which Chevrolet testers encountered in early shakedowns of the running prototypes. The tuned shockers helped make the ragtop a very tight package. This was not a feature unique to Camaro, having been used on Thunderbird and Lincoln convertibles as early as 1961, and on open 1965-69 Corvairs.

Camaro engines were shared with the concurrent Chevelle. Chevy's 230 cubic-inch six (140 bhp) was standard, with a 250-cid six (155 bhp) optional. Then came a long line of V-8s, commencing with 210- and 265-bhp 327s, and running on to the big 396-cid, 375-bhp L78 with four-barrel carburetors and 11:1 compression. This array of powerplants put Camaro firmly in the Mustang league. Here was a car the buyer could equip to suit his or her preferences—exactly what GM had in

E. M. "Pete" Estes (top) was Chevy general manager when the Camaro was introduced. He formally announced the new car's name (killing the long-assumed Panther moniker) in an unusual telephone press conference on June 29, 1966. Some three months later, Camaro (above) arrived.

15

mind. Incidentally, the Camaro appealed strongly to both sexes from the start: One out of every four buyers was female.

Chevrolet probably should have offered "courses in Camaro" to its customers in 1967—it certainly did to Chevy salesmen—so they could make sense of the enormous option list. It has been suggested that Detroit's practice of offering a cornucopia of optional extras, which began in the Sixties, contributed to its quality-control problems and sales losses to the imports, most of which came fully equipped. This may be true, but options were the way to go in 1967, and they helped trigger Camaro's early success. It was possible to build virtually any kind of car you wanted, as long as you had spent enough time reviewing the accessories sheets.

Months before its official introduction, the Camaro was the subject of extensive sneak previews and rumors, which probably stole some potential sales from Corvair. But by that time, GM was heavily committed to its Mustang-beater, and had started to downplay the rear-engined compact in the wake of widespread controversy over its safety.

The Camaro formally arrived in dealerships nationwide on September 21, 1966. Chevy explained that the new car's name was taken from an old French word meaning "companion" or "pal." Chevy even produced a photostat of an old French dictionary as proof. Despite its unfamiliar name, the Camaro sold well. For 1967, Chevrolet regained first rank in model year production, which it had lost to Ford in 1966. Volume was 2.2 million vehicles—and fully 10 percent were Camaros. Camaro didn't beat Mustang's sales, which were lower in '67 than in '65 and '66; they would drop even faster as Camaro began to hit its stride in 1968 and '69.

First-generation Camaros came in a choice of three levels: base, Rally Sport (RS), and Super Sport (SS 350); the latter powered by a special 295-bhp, 350-cid V-8. A Camaro SS 350 also included a heavy-duty suspension and distinctive "bumblebee" nose striping.

Although SS Camaros tend to attract the most attention from enthusiasts (second only to the Z-28), the Rally Sport option is our idea of the perfect trim scheme—neither too plain like the standard-trim version, nor too flashy like the SS. Briefly, it altered the car's appearance by means of concealed headlights set in a full-width grille, parking and backup lights mounted below the bumpers, lower bodyside moldings with black finish underneath, bright

Opposite: The '67 Camaro came in two bodystyles: notchback hardtop and convertible. The ragtop seen here listed at $2704 with the 140-bhp 230 cid six, but the 155-bhp Turbo-Thrift 250 (*middle, right*) added only a few dollars to the bottom line. (Owner: Ron Embleton) *This page:* Total '67 Camaro convertible output came to 25,141 units. Prices started at $2809 with the base V-8, but this well-equipped SS example cost at least $1000 more. Engine is the L48 350-cid Turbo-Fire, rated at 295 horsepower. (Owner: Ernest Gigliotti)

moldings around the wheel openings and along the beltline, and discreet "RS" emblems.

Stepping into (well, swinging into) a then-new Camaro brought an immediate impression of snugness—a trait of late-Sixties American coupes—with the back seat strictly "for emergency use only." Legroom for adults existed in name only, and riding in back for more than a dozen miles was guaranteed to wrinkle the passenger's designer jeans. Up front, the vinyl buckets of the Custom Interior, in particular, were well proportioned and comfortable. With no rake adjustment for the seatbacks, however, drivers with long legs might complain about lack of sufficient fore/aft seat travel. The big main instru-

ments were quite legible, though their curious cone-shaped lenses tended to produce a little distortion. All the controls fell readily to hand (as the British would say), obligatory in this sort of car.

The second-edition '68 Camaro was marked by only minor changes. Instant identification was provided by the new side marker lights mandated for all cars that year by the federal government. In common with other '68 Chevys (except Corvair), Camaro acquired flow-through "Astro Ventilation," thus doing away with "no-draft" quarter vents in the doors. It also adopted a peaked and silver (instead of flat and black) grille, and oblong (instead of round) parking lights. Taillights remained oblong, with separate red and

This page and opposite, top: Priced at $105.35, the 1967 RS (Regular Production Option Z-22) was basically a cosmetic package comprising hidden headlamps, square (instead of round) parking lights moved from the grille to spots under the bumper, full taillamps with separate under-bumper backup lights, and less functional items such as body pinstriping, bright rocker/drip rail/wheelarch moldings, black rocker bottoms, and RS badges. (Owner: Tom Bigelow)

white (backup) lenses on the standard versions, and a quartet of square red lenses for the RS, with separate backup lamps below the bumper.

Additional detailing made the 1968 SS 396 stand out from the rest of the line—specifically, a black-painted back panel and a new hood with fake air intakes. The SS package now included front disc brakes as standard equipment and offered a choice of three striping patterns, including a

"pulsating" set of color bands going from dark to light before merging into the body color. As the designation suggests, a big-block 396-cid engine was part of the deal (actually added in mid-1967). Otherwise, most RPOs (Regular Production Options) and the drivetrain lineup remained virtually the same as in '67.

The first generation changed considerably for 1969. This turned out to be an extra-long model year, because introduction of

the restyled 1970 Camaro was delayed until spring of that year. The engine lineup (see chart) was shuffled, as the 327 V-8 gave way to a new 307, and the 350-cid L65 unit replaced the high-performance 327. Four-wheel disc brakes, offered for '68 on the Z-28 mainly to give the racing versions better stopping power, now became optional for all models. Federal bumper regulations (then restricted to bumper height, not crash resistance) were

Camaro SS : One to go, with everything.

Camaro

GM

1968 Camaro
the "hugger" from Chevrolet CHEVROLET

Left: Camaro advertisements and promotional material emphasized optional power setups and handling finesse in 1967 and '68. The SS was aimed at driving enthusiasts, and featured the 350-cid V-8 plus stiffer springs and shocks, F70-14 tires on 14 x 7-inch wheels, "domed" hood with dual dummy exhaust vents, SS emblems, and a distinctive bumblebee stripe encircling the nose.

in effect, and Camaro was right up to date with optional Endura compressible bumpers. More vinyl roof colors were offered, along with two-tone paint.

The classic Mercedes-Benz 300SL sports car of the late Fifties and early Sixties has inspired the design of many Detroit cars, some of which actually benefited from its example. Camaro certainly did: its front wheel cutouts were more square, and gained speed streaks echoing the heavily emphasized "brows" of the Mercedes. These swept straight back from both front and rear wheels to give a look of forward motion. (One 300SL item evidently did *not* enter production: simulated air vents behind the front wheels. This also was proposed for the '68 Rally Sport and appeared in some factory photographs, but it was likely scrapped at the last minute.)

The "face" of the '69 car was also altered as much as possible without major sheet-metal changes. The grille was set farther back in its opening, more strongly vee'd than before, and got a big eggcrate pattern. On Rally Sport models, the headlamps remained hidden when off, but their covers now had three glass "ribs," which allowed some light to shine through if the hoods failed to retract.

Forced to make a choice, we'd pick the 1967 model as the best-styled Camaro

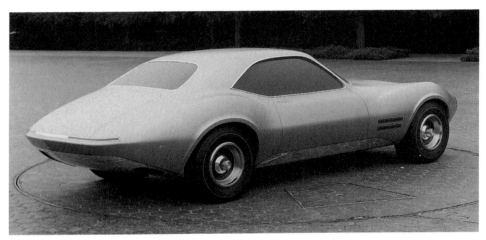

Camaro's first generation had not yet bowed when GM stylists were already at work on refinements and changes. The clays seen here date from August of 1966, the drawings from January of '67.

from the early years. Detroit has frequently been criticized for tampering with a basically good design, just for the sake of change. The Camaro's cosmetic surgery for 1968 and '69 was minor, to be sure, but unnecessary. Despite Bill Mitchell's suggestion that this was a committee design, most observers liked it fine — especially the convertible. (The committee must have been a good one.) Sporty, yet practical for a car of its day, it's still well-suited for today's driving conditions. And who would complain about this kind of performance combined with 22 miles to a gallon of regular?

Around the time of its debut, the Camaro was sometimes described by automotive journalists as a Detroit alternative to imported sports cars. Camaro, after all, offered a number of the features that might tempt someone seeking an MG or Triumph, with the bonus of extra room for passengers and luggage. Yet oddly enough, hardly anybody bothered to test one equipped along the lines of a European GT. Instead, the emphasis in auto magazines (and in GM showrooms) focused almost solely on the powerhouse V-8s.

Lack of publicity didn't hurt the six-cylinder cars — at least in the beginning. From 50,000 to 65,000 sixes were sold each year during the first generation, accounting for about one in every four sales. A properly set-up six-cylinder Camaro made a mighty pleasing package, whether in coupe or convertible form. And it didn't cost much, either. A $3300 price tag ranked as a pretty good deal back in 1967.

Chevrolet offered a choice of two inline sixes. The optional 250-cid six, with 155 horsepower, provided a welcome performance boost over the standard 230-cid unit, at little cost in fuel mileage. Priced at only $26.35 extra back in '67, the 250 was worth its weight in gold. Its torque peak came at a mere 1600 rpm, so you wouldn't have to spend a lot of time in the lower gears to get the most out of it. Vastly underrated in its time, it was built to be an unbreakable, slow-revving engine with a long life. This willing six-cylinder was hooked to an all-synchro gearbox with four ratios, fairly widely spaced. An optional 3.55:1 "performance" rear axle ratio could be ordered, instead of the standard 3.08:1 or "economy" 2.73:1 cog. While the 3.55 axle cut down a little on top speed, it provided low-end performance that rivaled that of, say, a Triumph TR4. And, considering that Camaro weighed about 3000 pounds (19.4

Chevy listed no fewer than four 396 big-block V-8s for the '68 Camaro: L34, L35, L78, and L89, ranging in horsepower from 325 to 375. The yellow SS 396 (*above*) storms along with the L35, which boasted 10.25:1 compression and 325 horses, mated to a THM 400 automatic. (Owner: Ramshead Auto Collection) Camaro was little changed for '68, but the sidemarker lights (*left*) were one telltale clue. (Owner: Robert R. Lotito) The lack of ventwings (*below left*) was another. Cockpit (*below*) remains handsome today. (Owner: Robert Francek)

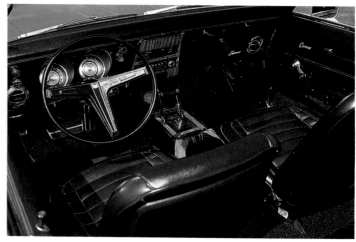

Opposite: The '69 Camaro with the Rally Sport option received front fender badges and RS lettering in the center of the grille. This example also sports the Cowl-Induction hood. (Owner: Mike D'Amico) *Above:* This '69 hardtop runs with a 230-cid six and automatic. Though ignored by the press, the six-cylinder Camaros handled beautifully. (Owner: Rob Embleton)

Camaro Engine Options 1967-69

Engine	cid	bore x stroke (in.)	bhp @ rpm (gross)	C.R. (:1)	carb (bbls)	1967	Available 1968	1969
six	230	3.88 x 3.25	140 @ 4400	8.5	1	x	x	x
six	250	3.88 x 3.53	155 @ 4200	8.5	1	x	x	x
V-8	302	4.00 x 3.01	290 @ 5800	11.0	4	x	x	x
V-8	307	3.88 x 3.25	200 @ 4600	9.0	2			x
V-8	327	4.00 x 3.25	210 @ 4600	8.75	2	x	x	x
V-8	327	4.00 x 3.25	275 @ 4800	10.0	4	x	x	
V-8	350	4.00 x 3.48	250 @ 4800	9.0	2			x
V-8	350	4.00 x 3.48	295 @ 4800	10.25	4	x	x	
V-8	350	4.00 x 3.48	300 @ 4800	10.25	4			x
V-8	396	4.09 x 3.76	325 @ 4800	10.25	4	x	x	x
V-8	396	4.09 x 3.76	350 @ 5200	10.25	4			x
V-8	396	4.09 x 3.76	375 @ 5600	11.0	4	x	x	x
V-8	427	4.25 x 3.76	425 @ 5600	11.0	3 x 2			x

pounds per horsepower), it had better-than-acceptable acceleration in this form. Repeated 0-60 mph runs hardly ever varied between 12.5 and 14 seconds—and this with a *six*. In standing-start quarter-mile times, the Camaro matched the contemporary Triumph almost exactly.

We rank the six-cylinder Sport Coupe highly for those enthusiasts who want an interesting, stylish collectible that can be treated as an everyday car, which still offers a practical combination of performance, economy, and dependability. One of the few road tests of a six-cylinder model, conducted by *Motor Trend* in 1968, summed up its capability very well: "The 250-cube 6 has enough torque to bowl over banana trees, and will even do a decent job on the highway scene. [It] represents a great little integrated driving package—a welcome relief from the power-mad supercar whose acceleration response is so intense and overwhelming that it takes on the character of a partially controlled ballistic missile. . . . The machine is so well balanced. . . . Not a wide-ovalled tire or a stiff suspension-that-feels-like-advanced-rigor mortis-has-set-in anywhere,

and the little machine fairly flys [sic] through the esses."

As for equipment, no more than 38,000 of the first-generation Camaros were ordered with air conditioning, which wasn't even offered on six-cylinder models.

We can't say much that's negative about the first Camaros, apart from the fact that the standard all-drum brake system was inadequate for anything except gentle, routine driving—a complaint that lingered into the next generation. Convertibles came with 11-inch front drums instead of the coupe's 9.5-inchers, but this wasn't enough. As a minimum, we would have recommended sintered metallic linings ($37.90) or, better yet, ventilated front discs ($79), with or without vacuum assist ($42.15). Power was also available for drum brake setups, but did nothing except make them too pedal-sensitive.

Some drivers also found the manual steering to be too slow. A 28:1 ratio was specified for the convertible, compared to 24:1 on coupes, but even that didn't offer enough improvement. Chevy had a couple of cures. A customer could order the regular power steering option ($84.30),

Above and opposite, top: The '69 Camaro convertible with the standard 200-bhp 307 V-8 listed at $2940. The $311.75 SS group upped that to a 300-bhp 350. Beyond that, the buyer could order a 396 V-8, seen here in L78 form, good for 375 bhp at 5600 rpm. (Owner: Charley Lillard) *Opposite, bottom:* Camaro had paced the Indy 500 in 1967, and did so again in '69. This '69 hardtop sports the look and 350 V-8 of that year's pace car-replica ragtops. (Owner: Steven Knutsen)

which reduced the gearing to 17.5:1; there was also the short-spindle-arm N44 quick-ratio steering, available with (15.6:1 ratio) or without (18:1) power assist ($15.80). Typically, Chevy had an option that could satisfy almost any owner's requirements.

The late Sixties saw the height of the ponycar craze, as all the major makers brought out short-wheelbase, sporty compacts that held two passengers plus two-in-a-pinch (almost literally). Everyone was after the market that the Mustang had exploited so early—Mercury with its Cougar, Dodge with its Charger, Rambler with its ill-advised Marlin, Pontiac with its Firebird, and Plymouth with its Barracuda. The latter was fully restyled for 1967,

25

Chevy built 3675 pace car replica convertibles for 1969. Besides bold paint, stripes and 350 V-8, they came with the RS/SS packages, Turbo Hydra-Matic, and Cowl-Induction hood. (Owner: Sandy D'Amico)

adding another low-priced challenge to the Mustang, though it didn't approach either Mustang or Camaro in sales. Most interesting is how Camaro production remained almost stable from 1967 through 1969, while Mustang figures dropped steadily. By the end of the decade, Camaro was rapidly closing on the original ponycar:

Model Year	Camaro	Mustang	Barracuda
1967	220,917	472,121	62,534
1968	235,151	317,404	45,412
1969	243,095	299,824	32,987

Sales figures for cars like the Firebird and Cougar show that all other challengers were merely chipping away at Mustang, while Camaro gamely held its own profitable market share.

How did the "low-priced three's" ponycar contenders compare? Camaro and Barracuda were certainly more up to date in styling than the Mustang, yet none of the three had a clear performance lead over the others. Each car was, as *Road & Track* magazine put it, "basically a compact sedan with a stylish body, with all the virtues and vices of the typical American sedan. True, each can be ordered with things like improved steering, braking, handling, instrumentation, etc. But in each case these things aren't a fundamental part of the concept. None of them offers anywhere near the best present-day standards in braking or handling. Each of them is a very plain car in standard form, and the options necessary to bring them up to the relatively simple form in which we tested them make them fairly expensive cars."

Missing in this analysis is the fact that European 2+2s were designed for the needs of a very much smaller, more highly specialized market. As a result, the volume necessary for a firm like Ferrari or Mercedes-Benz to break even on such expensive products was a lot lower than for a mass-production U.S. model.

Camaro was selected to pace the Indianapolis 500 twice in three years— 1967 and 1969—so it must have impressed some people who liked to go fast. But not the editors of *Road & Track:* "The Camaro is, frankly, a disappointment. Chevrolet has been an engineering leader in the past, and we assumed that if they had years in which to develop a car, they might reasonably be expected to surpass the Mustang rather than just equal it."

In truth, that's just what happened. As proof, consider the development of the Z-28, as described in the following pages.

Don Yenko did for Camaro what Carroll Shelby did for Mustang. Result: factory installation of the L72 427 V-8, plus Z-28 suspension, close-ratio Muncie four-speed, and 140-mph speedo. (Owner: Jerry Buczkowski)

Chapter Two

Birth of the Z-28: Wizards at Work

Seldom in automotive history has a name that stands for essentially nothing come to mean so much. We refer to the Camaro Z-28, a designation that signified nothing other than the ordering code for a new race-bred option package, but which quickly came to symbolize slammed-into-the-seat acceleration and acutely precise handling. And, to some, a bone-crushing ride on anything other than a smooth pavement. The famous RPO (Regular Production Option) code, incidentally, was variously printed with a hyphen (Z-28) or a slash (Z/28), or with no punctuation at all (Z28). By the time of the third generation in the 1980s, at least, "Z28" was the customary style, though some publications continued to employ a hyphen.

One of the best descriptions of the Camaro Z-28 came from an unlikely quarter back in April 1967. "When is a sports car not a sports car?" asked the Australian magazine *Sports Car World*. "If you answered 'when it's a yank tank' you could be wrong."

The editors went on to say that what Americans called sports cars—and this included the Z-28—were not appreciated by enthusiasts "Down Under." This occurred "because we don't understand them. . . . Australians still have a deep resentment of [such cars] because our standard of living

Z-28, an essentially meaningless
Camaro ordering code, quickly came
to stand for great looks and
storming performance.

and car purchasing power hasn't yet permitted us to indulge in it. . . . We hurt a lot of purists when we ran a funny test a few years back between the respective 2-plus-2s of the variously distinguished houses of Ferrari and Pontiac. The big cumbersome Ponty went round a test track in the hands of an independent pilot as quick as the Ferrari. . . . We're not saying a Pontiac is a Ferrari because they're designed for two infinitely different purposes and bred from

far removed backgrounds. But we are bound to point out that the American sporting machine is not the unsophisticated mechanical garbage can that most people would like to believe."

The editors went on to note that their test Camaro (merely a 350 SS, not a Z-28) had "acceleration to match the best of Europe, braking of a high order, and handling that was surprisingly equal with some top Continental machinery on the

Just 602 Z-28s were produced for 1967, but the number rose to 7199 in '68, and to 19,014 for 1969. The '69 Z-28 (*below*) sailed into the model year with new styling, but basically the same mechanicals as before. The original performance idea of Chevy engineer Vince Piggins had borne glorious fruit. (Owner: Nick D'Amico)

faster bends." If a Camaro was slower on tight bends, well, you have to remember that twisty, crowded roads heavily influenced European auto engineering, while America was a land of wide-open spaces.

Finally, the editors declared, "Americans are probably more in contact with the world of sporting motoring than any other nationality in the world: after all they own half the world's sports cars, and they are the export territory for about 90 percent of those very cars produced on the Continent. If you want to get really basic you'll have to realize that America is probably the only reason half those European concessionaires [manufacturers] are in business!"

Chevy's Z-28 was precisely the kind of car these perceptive Aussies were talking about. By European standards it didn't seem like much. This was no exotic, hand-built *gran turismo* with sophisticated engineering, built at the rate of one or ten a day. Instead, the "Z" was a conventional design based on mass-produced components right off the GM parts shelf. The genius of the design lay in the fact that all of its seemingly ordinary pieces worked so impressively well together. This is why the Z-28 became what Camaro historian

This page and opposite: The rarest and most desirable '67 Camaros were the Z-28s—only 602 were built. Inspired by the SCAA Trans-Am races, they ran with a 302.4-cid Turbo Fire V-8 rated at 290 horses, but 400 was probably more like it. (Owner: Paul McGuire)

Michael Lamm termed a "Legend in its Own Time." Truly magical.

If one man deserves credit for the Z-28 concept, it would certainly be Vincent W. Piggins, who had been a Chevrolet engineer since 1956. "After Ford released the Mustang," Piggins explained, "they had about two years on us before Chevrolet could get the Camaro into the 1967 product line. I felt in my activity, which deals with product promotion and how to get the most promotional mileage from a car from the performance standpoint, that we needed to develop a performance image for the Camaro that would be superior to the Mustang's.

"Along comes SCCA in creating the Trans-Am sedan racing class for professional drivers in 1966, aimed for the 1967 season. I made it a point to have several discussions with SCCA officials—notably Jim Kaser, John Bishop and Tracy Byrd—and one thing led to another. I suggested a vehicle that would fit this class and, I believe—supported by what Chevrolet might do with the Camaro—it gave them the heart to push ahead and make up the rules, regulations and so forth for the Trans-Am series. I feel this was really the creation of the Trans-Am as we know it."

As originally devised, the Trans-Am series had two classes. The one that's relevant here applied to "sedans" with a 116-inch wheelbase or less, and engine displacement not exceeding 305 cubic inches. Because Camaro had a rear seat, it qualified as a "sedan."

To be eligible, a car had to be produced in quantities of at least 1000 units in any model year. Though Chevrolet sold only 602 of the 1967-model Z-28s, it met the minimum production requirement by homologating the standard 350-cid Camaro under *Federacion International d'Automobile* (FIA) Group I rules, then qualifying the car with the Z-28 *option* under Group II. Clever.

The original scheme for the Z-28, according to Piggins, was to combine the following components in one package: F41 heavy-duty suspension, front disc brakes, metallic-lined rear drum brakes, 24:1 quick-ratio steering gear, Corvette 15 x 6 wheels with 7.75 x 15 tires, and a special hood with functional air intake. Together, these transformed a stock Camaro into a Z-28. The drivetrain would have comprised GM's close-ratio four-speed manual transmission and the 283-cid V-8, but Piggins had a "better idea."

"While we were driving the [prototype], I mentioned that we'd put the 283 into it because we'd built that size engine before. But I suggested that it might be a lot better to take the 327 block and put the 283 crank into it, giving us 4 x 3 bore and stroke. That would put displacement at 302.4 cid, just under the SCCA's 305 limit. So [Chevrolet general manager Elliot M. "Pete"] Estes immediately agreed, especially being an engineer and knowing the potential this car could have."

Chevrolet rated the 302's output at a very conservative 290 brake horsepower, with 290 foot-pounds of torque. This figure, as one magazine put it, was "laughable.... Four hundred [horsepower] comes much nearer the truth. This is a fistful of energy any way you dissect it. A 4-inch bore allows generously large valves, and the short 3-inch stroke keeps friction low and lets this engine wind to 7200 without missing a beat." Conservatively speaking, standard tune gave what we'd estimate to be at least 350 bhp.

Complementing the 283 crank in the 327 block was a huge, four-barrel Holley carburetor on a special oversize manifold with large ports and valves, along with a 346-degree-duration high-lift cam (with 118 degrees of overlap) and cast-iron headers. Though closely related to the

This page and opposite: For 1968 the $400 Z-28 option was usually combined with RS gear, as on the '68s seen here. Chevy advertised the Z-28 as the "Closest thing to a Corvette yet," and no wonder, considering the 302 V-8 and 800 cfm Holley four-barrel carburetor. (Owner: Donald R. Crile)

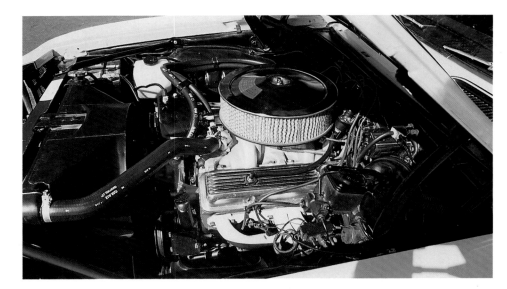

This page and opposite: By 1969, the Z-28 had sped away with the Trans-Am racing crown for the second year in a row, earning a reputation as a car with performance as hot as its looks. The hood scoop pulled air from a high-turbulence area just ahead of the windshield. The 302 was switched to four-bolt mains, while rolling stock was slimmed to six-inch-wide rims wearing E70-15 Firestone Sports Car 200 high-performance tires. (Owner: Nick D'Amico)

283's standard cast-iron crankshaft, the Z-28's strong forged-steel crank wasn't identical. All of this formed the very heart of the Z-28's motive power—and it was tremendous.

With a compression ratio of 11:1, gas of the highest octane was mandatory. In later days of low-calorie unleaded, you'd either have to fill a Z-28 at the local airport, or carry cans of octane additive. Plenty of it, too, as typical mileage ranged between eight and 14 mpg, averaging about 12.5. The noisy engine idled at 900 rpm—lumpily and uneasily to be sure (it would rather be winding up to 4000-plus).

People who wanted a Z-28 in the early days—and they did, in larger numbers than Chevy expected—could have the most basic set-up for about $3800. The Z-28

option itself (302 V-8, F41 suspension, quick steering, special trim, and Rally wheels with wide-tread GT tires) added only about $400 to the under-$3000 base price of a plain-Jane Camaro coupe. But to get this hot package, you *also* had to order front disc brakes with power assist and one of three available four-speed manual transmissions. This boosted the price by another $300-$400. And that was for the "economy special."

No one could buy a Z-28 in convertible form, but Chevrolet dangled an impressive array of other extra-cost items to tempt tire-kickers: Rally Sport package, Positraction, sintered metallic rear brake drum linings, headers, ram-air system, and fiberglass rear spoiler. The most expensive option, offered for 1968-69, was a pair of

600-cfm four-barrel Holley carburetors mounted on a special manifold—$500 plus dealer installation.

So, it wasn't impossible to work a Z-28 up to the $5000 level. Even so, this was not considered outlandish by those interested in winning races, though it did turn off a few would-be owners of street machines.

Winning races was Chevy's primary aim in developing the Z-28. The first 25 cars were built before mid-January 1967 (contrary to some rumors, the Z-28 was *not* a "1967½" introduction). Most were sent to dealerships with an active involvement in racing, such as the Don Yenko and Roger Penske outlets in Pennsylvania, Nickey Chevrolet in Chicago, and Ron Tonkin in Portland, Oregon. Most of these dealers began preparing and entering the cars in

Trans-Am competition. In due course the exercise paid off: Camaro was champion in the over-2-liter class for both 1968 and '69. This meant—to Chevrolet's unmitigated delight—that Mustang *wasn't*.

Though many driver/dealer duos drove to success with the Z-28, the twosome that really stood out was composed of Mark Donohue and Roger Penske. Penske, a prominent Pennsylvania Chevy agent with several dealerships, was a fine racing driver in his own right, and had known Donohue since their early SCCA days. Roger asked Mark to drive a Camaro for him in the 1967 Trans-Am campaign. Due to what must have been a misunderstanding, Donohue was asked to spec-out the suspension, about which he knew nothing. (The engine prep, by Traco of California, was beyond criticism; its engines just wouldn't stop.) Due to Donohue's inexperience, the team's initial appearances at Daytona and Sebring were marred by handling woes. What's more, the cars didn't brake well. Donohue eked out a second-in-class at Sebring, but the victory went to Mustang.

At this point Chevrolet Research &

Development stepped in, determined to make the Z-28 a winner. The braking problem was solved by reversing the lines from their stock position, allowing the master cylinder's larger piston to work the front discs rather than the rear drums. Still, the Penske car did not fare well in its next two outings, so Chevrolet invited Donohue and car to the Milford, Michigan, proving grounds for a thorough going-over.

There, the Camaro went through a tremendous number of tests, many made with sophisticated sensors attached to the suspension, drivetrain, and body. Computer analysis helped the engineers zero in on the weak points. Two things were learned: First, the body needed strengthening to prevent flex that was interfering with suspension geometry; second, the right rear traction bar also upset suspension geometry (it was later removed).

Remaining suspension problems were thrashed out in practice before the next event at Upper Marlboro, Maryland. Chevrolet R&D sent a discreetly marked van—with Pennsylvania license plates—loaded with enough spare parts, tools, and equipment to handle any possible need.

Various suspension changes were made, then Donohue would test each one out on the track. After an exhausting number of trial-and-error evaluations, followed by a complete pre-race teardown, the Penske Z-28 was at last ready. The work paid off: Camaro scored its first victory in Trans-Am competition, with a 63-mph average. That wouldn't sound like much unless you'd driven the narrow, twisty Marlboro course. It was an impressive win all right, and Donohue began to smile again.

Not much time remained for the Z-28 to recover the 1967 series, however, and the loss of the number-one machine in a road accident before a California race cost more time while a back-up car was keyed-in. Still, Donohue won the last two races of the season—a portent of things to come.

During preparation for the 1968 battles, the Z-28 racing program began to take on an other-worldly aspect. If Ford folk could have looked in on it, they might have been discouraged—yet impressed—by the amount of technology being mustered by their rich and determined rivals. While the Penske team developed its '68 cars based on seat-of-the-pants experiences from the

36

This page and opposite: Dealer-installed, $500 stock option of dual four-barrel carbs (*left*) combined with the "cold air" hood to turn the '69 Z-28 into a real screamer. The hidden headlamps (*above*) that came with the Rally Sport option for '69 gained triple glass windows for "flash to pass" signaling. (Owner: Charley Lillard)

year before, GM was at work on some far-out engineering: independent rear suspension (irs), four-wheel disc brakes, and quick-release (by engine vacuum) disc pads to speed up pit stops. Of these, only the irs was discarded, because its effect on the Camaro's actual track performance was negligible. And as if that weren't enough,

Chevy came up with something that could actually monitor the car *while it was being raced:* a "telemetry van," loaded with computers. Hooked into radiotelephone links with the car, they recorded every physical action/reaction that went on throughout the race.

The "telemetry van" was an imaginative

stroke that proved crucial to the 1968 racing effort. With the data it supplied, engineers constructed computer models of the car. Then, by tinkering with suspension, brakes, and other components, they could design—again by computer—an optimum mechanical and handling package to fit any race course. Ford fanciers could have staged a protest under the banner "Unfair to Mustang."

The kick-off event for the '68 Trans-Am series was at Daytona, but again proved a disappointment for Camaro. The team finished second-in-class due to cracked heads and time lost in subsequent pit stops. At Sebring, though, Penske and GM couldn't have asked for more. The two team cars finished third and fourth overall, trailing only a pair of 911 Porsches, and took the GT class one-two. After that, Camaro virtually romped through the rest of the year, winning nine of the remaining 11 races to capture the over-2-liter crown.

After considerable work with the "telemetry van," the following year brought two new Penske cars. The story was a repeat: eight out of 12 Trans-Am events won by Camaro, which held the title for the second straight year. Mustang had been defeated.

However, 1970 was a gloomy year for Z-fans. Penske and Donohue were spirited away by American Motors, and were soon setting records with Javelins. The new second-generation Camaro didn't go on sale until the season was well under way, and by then it was too late for anyone to do much with it—even someone with Donohue's brand of skill and persistence. No matter, the Z-28 had made its point. Thanks to the incredible devotion of Penske, Donohue, and Chevrolet R&D, it had become, in just two short years, a performance legend.

Changes in the Z-28's specifications for 1968 and '69 were slight but important. For 1968, the engine stayed basically the same, but crankshaft bearing diameters were enlarged, and the special dual four-barrel manifold ($500 plus dealer installation) appeared. Four-wheel disc brakes, giving a total swept lining area of 461.2 square inches, were offered as a "service option" late in the model year. Quick steering (21.4:1 ratio) became standard, and an even quicker ratio (17.9:1) was available at extra cost. Comparable gearing was on hand for power assist. An expanded list of competition options included special steering components, plastic racing bucket seats, air dams, and rear spoilers. Another useful goody was a double-thick front anti-sway bar to replace the standard item. Five-leaf rear springs with heavy-duty staggered shocks became standard Z-28 hardware, and that tricky righthand radius rod was deleted.

The production '69 model, last of the first-generation cars, was distinguished by the addition of a "cold-air" hood, featuring a rear-facing scoop angled to catch the wind at a point of maximum turbulence. The 302 V-8 switched to four-bolt mains, while the 15-inch chrome Rally wheels slimmed down from seven to six inches in width. In place of the standard Goodyear tires came Firestone E70-15 Sports Car 200s. Finally, the four-wheel disc brakes became a Regular Production Option for '69 instead of a "service option" (which meant a few of them reached the street, but not many).

Small but significant styling changes occurred on all Camaros that year. While the 1967-68 car was smooth and clean, the '69 was bulkier and more aggressive. A no-nonsense eggcrate grille, vee'd out in the middle, combined with crisp, creased "eyebrows" over the wheel openings and pressed-in hashmarks ahead of the rear wheels to suggest purpose and performance. On Z-28s, this more extroverted look was carried to its logical conclusion. A big air dam rode under the wide-mouth grille. The huge cold-air intake swept back from the front of the hood, which was adorned with broad racing stripes. Two more stripes rode the rear deck, which was capped by a prominent spoiler.

Some aspects of the '69 interior lagged behind the 1967-68 models. Headrests, dictated by that year's safety regulations, tended to obstruct over-the-shoulder vision; fortunately, the headrests were removable. The redesigned dash dispensed with the original, simple twin-dial layout and substituted a slightly curved arrangement with round instruments in square housings. This concoction, by Don Schwartz's interior studio at GM Styling, may have been prompted by the arrival of flow-through ventilation the year before, although the air vents were first incorporated without changing the original dash design. With the two-spoke steering wheel, instruments could be hard to read. Auxiliary gauges, again carried ahead of the shifter atop the plastic console, were even harder to spot, especially when the driver allowed the Z-28 to do what it did best.

The '69 Z-car looks—and is—mean, hairy, rugged, and ready to devour just about any Mustang. While other sporty cars followed the trend toward comfort and compromise in 1969, the Z-28 became even more of a hot-blooded thoroughbred—a racing car suitable for occasional use on the street. Back then, a lot of people were surprised the beast was actually legal.

Chevrolet general manager "Pete" Estes was bullish about the '69 Camaro Z-28. "We only planned on selling about 400 in 1968," he said, "but instead, we had 7000 orders. Boy, there are kids out there, and they have money. And when they hear how Mark Donohue cleans up in Trans-Am with a Z-28 they've just *got* to have one for themselves. In 1969 we plan to sell 27,000. Can you imagine? 27,000!"

Sales figures were not quite that rosy, but the 1969 model does rank as all-time Z-28 leader: 19,014 were built, against 7199 of the '68 version and 602 of the '67s. Small wonder: The '69 was the very essence of the whole Z-28 idea. Not until 1977 did production again even come close, when 14,349 copies of a much detuned and considerably tamer Z-28 were built. The ponycar craze had peaked by 1969, then plummeted in the early Seventies, bottoming out with the oil crisis of 1973-74.

How fast was the Z-28, really? Well, Smokey Yunick took his own car to Bonneville in October 1967, after having been denied entry to the final Trans-Am race. His drivers included Mickey Thompson, Curtis Turner, and Bunkie Blackburn. Thompson managed a flying mile at 174.344 mph, beating the Class C American Stock record set in 1963 (by a Studebaker GT Hawk) by almost 30 mph. Yunick managed to blow his engine in the standing 10-kilometer runs, but after he put it back together he broke another record by running for 12 hours straight at over 140 mph. All told, Yunick's Z-28 shattered 259 Class B, Class C, and Unlimited world speed records. (Class B runs were made with the same car powered by an L78 396 V-8, which gave a top speed of 183.486 mph—beating a record set by Pontiac in 1962.)

Street Zs weren't tuned to this level, of

Street Z-28s were not tuned to the same performance level as their racing counterparts, of course, but they could give most other cars fits in the stoplight derby. All that potential for speed brought better brakes for '69: four-wheel discs offered as a Regular Production Option. This '69 Z-28 (*above and opposite*) is RS-equipped. (Owner: Tony D'Amico)

course, but they proved mighty impressive nonetheless. *Car and Driver* magazine tested one with the hairy, twin four-barrel set-up, recording 0-60 mph acceleration in 5.3 seconds, and a stunning quarter-mile time of 13.77 seconds at 107.39 mph—real drag race stuff. Of course, they also had the advantage of having Sam Posey to do the driving.

Motor Trend also drove a 1969 Z-car with the optional dual four-barrel Holley carburetors. "Wild as it may have been for 1968," they declared, "—eliciting comments like, 'Man, sounds great!' just while idling at a stoplight—it has become downright immoral for 1969.... The cam rocks the Z-28 and furls brows of adjacent motorists."

A touch of the accelerator—and it had better be a touch because of the hair-trigger throttle linkage—was all that was necessary to launch this projectile. Even the standard four-barrel induction system delivered 0-60 mph times in the low-7s or high-6s. Standing-start quarter-mile time was under 15 seconds, resulting in over 100 mph. To produce those figures, the drill was to rev the engine to 3500 rpm, then pop the clutch. With a numerically low axle ratio installed, the '69 Z-28 was capable of close to 150 mph flat out, even though the speedometer read only to 120 mph.

One of the Z-28's drawbacks was anemic low-end response—not unexpected in a semi-competition machine designed for high revs. Torque peaked at a lofty 4200 rpm, and not much happened below that, which is why the powerplant had to rev so high to get underway.

Car Life magazine noted in 1968 that the Z-28 was one machine that needed its four forward gears. In most cars of its type, said the writer, torque peaked too far down the scale to make four speeds really necessary. But the Z had all kinds of muscle

available, and was eager to spin over that 4000-rpm mark.

Clutch pressure was surprisingly light. Chevrolet deserves credit here, for this was a hefty, 11-inch-diameter clutch with spring pressures over 2700 pounds—larger and stronger even than the one used with the 396 V-8. Yet anyone could manage the Z-28's clutch, most without stomping very hard on the pedal.

When it came to handling, the Z-28 was definitely tighter and more grippy than a standard 1969 Camaro, although the suspension specs weren't all that different. The Z's front spring rates were the same as those of the 327-equipped models, while the rear rates were higher by approximately 125 percent than on the 396 versions. Naturally, all the big-engined Camaros used multi-leaf, instead of single-leaf, rear springs. Why? Because there would be no way to keep the back end on the ground with the standard setup.

Harshness on the road had to be expected. This was a competition machine first, and a road car a *very* distant second, with a ride too stiff for the average driver. Brake fade could be a problem, too, after the second or third hard stop. Trouble is, severe brake use could be commonplace given the car's tremendous performance—at least it probably could be when cars like the Z-28 were driven daily instead of just to the occasional meet or competition. It's easy to understand why brake problems troubled the Trans-Am team from time to time, and why GM had to come up with four-wheel discs as a service option.

Behind the wheel, you'd constantly be aware that this was a Detroit car, not a European one. The high beltline, low seating position, and enveloping dash created a "sitting-in-a-bathtub" feeling. The hood appeared enormous. And after all, this *was* a big car, judged by latter-day standards. There was a lot of mass to fling

around at any speed, let alone at the vein-popping velocities this car could achieve. These factors, combined with poor gas mileage, raucous engine, and weak low-rpm response, made the Z-28 very much a special-purpose car.

That said, the Z's performance at really high speeds was something to stir the blood. *Road & Track* magazine perhaps put it best in its original test of a '68 model: "With its wide tires the Z-28 is a stable, near-neutral car that has no trouble setting excellent lap times around any reasonably smooth course. The trick with a car like this, with all that torque available in the right gear, is to find that point where you're using just enough throttle to get it around a turn neutrally rather than plowing or spinning out."

How did the Z-car compare to its arch-rival, the Shelby-Mustang GT-350? We think the Camaro was a tad more comfortable—an attribute that's usually been ignored in evaluating cars like this. Camaro's driving position seemed more relaxed, with more room behind the wheel than in a Shelby. That included lots of elbow room for the arm flinging required to careen at 90-plus through corners marked "45 mph." And a person would be sorely tempted back then to do that a lot in a Z-28.

No matter how you look at it—street, drag race, Trans-Am, or Salt Flats—the Z-28 was a tremendous high-performance machine. It remains so to this day, especially when compared to the anemic, so-called performance cars of the Seventies, which reflected the nation's changing priorities. Even though performance has since enjoyed a comeback, there will probably never again be such a rip-snorting, fire-breathing, hairy-chested grand tourer as this. The Z-28s that survived have long since become collectors' prizes—artifacts of a memorable age that now seems long ago and far away.

1969 Z-28 SPECIFICATIONS

DIMENSIONS

Wheelbase: 108 inches. **Length:** 184.6 inches. **Width:** 72.3 inches. **Height:** 50.9 inches. **Weight:** 3300 pounds.

ENGINE

Type: ohv 90-degree V-8. **Bore-and-Stroke:** 4.00 x 3.00 inches. **Displacement:** 302 cubic inches. **Estimated bhp:** 350 @ 5300 rpm **Estimated torque:** 325 foot-pounds @ 4200 rpm.

CHASSIS

Unitized body/chassis. **Front suspension:** independent with unequal-length A-arms, coil springs, tubular shocks and anti-roll bar. **Rear sus-**

pension: live axle with semi-elliptic leaf springs and tubular shocks.
Brakes: disc front, drum rear, 332 square inches total swept area.
Steering: integral-assist recirculating ball gear with parallelogram linkage, 17:1 overall ratio, 2.8 turns lock-to-lock, 36.5 ft. turning circle.

PERFORMANCE

0-30 mph: 3.5 seconds.
0-60 mph: 7.2 seconds.
0-80 mph: 10.3 seconds.
Standing start quarter mile: 14.8 seconds @ 103 mph.
Speeds in gears (mph): 63 (1st), 87 (2nd), 115 (3rd), estimated 135 (4th).
Fuel consumption: 8-14 mpg, average 12.5.

Chapter Three

Second Generation: The Mitchell Legacy

Faced by increasingly tough federal regulations, Camaro's second generation finessed its way to sales success by emphasizing the sleek and sexy styling created under the aegis of Bill Mitchell.

S ome good cars fade fast. Others last a long while. Several of the best, as it happened, have come from Chevrolet, including the stylish and long-lived follow-up to the original Camaro.

So different and yet so similar, the second-generation Camaro appeared in the spring of 1970. Remarkably, it was still in production over 11 years later—and in basically the same form. It was predominantly a designer's car. Fast ones were built, of course, as we shall see. But a double-barreled assault from federal regulations and a changing market made the 1970-81 Camaros considerably tamer than their hell-bent-for-leather predecessors. Styling, not performance, is what made the post-1969 generation a classic in its own time. And, though many people were responsible for its smooth good looks, all the final decisions were made by just one individual: William L. Mitchell.

Probably more than anyone else in Detroit, Bill Mitchell influenced the way cars looked in the Sixties, Seventies, and Eighties—even those that were not General Motors products. In fact, it's fair to say that Mitchell indirectly contributed to the lines of cars as far removed from Camaro as the Ford Granada and Chrysler Cordoba—perhaps more than Dearborn or Highland Park would be willing to admit. Over the years, both competitors tried to one-up GM Styling and the "gospel" according to Mitchell. Sometimes they succeeded. Many times they did not.

Marketing expert Theodore MacManus once said of Cadillac, "If the leader leads, he remains the leader." GM set the trends

for Detroit styling for some 20 years, until the advent of aero bodies as the imports gained a firm foothold in the Eighties. And even then, the GM influence hardly evaporated.

MacManus also said that leaders have their detractors. Bill Mitchell certainly had his share. A few were other designers, some of them also-rans in a profession he dominated for 20 years and influenced for 40. Others were second-guessers from outside the auto industry. Based on the chrome-covered American glitter wagons they saw, they concluded that no Detroit stylist was worth a nickel. But being a fair critic requires thorough knowledge of an individual designer and his work, plus an appreciation for the enormous pressure automotive stylists feel from sales people

and higher management. These critics did not have such knowledge.

Then there were those who simply didn't like Bill Mitchell's personal style. One English writer observed, "His round body clad in bright scarlet or mylar chrome-coated leathers, astride one of his adolescent fantasy motorcycles, is enough to force a guffaw from Samuel Beckett." Rubbish, to use an appropriate English expression. Bill Mitchell's choice in dress or personal transportation had no bearing on his professional competence, which was obvious and considerable.

When Mitchell relieved Harley Earl as chief of GM Design in 1958, he stepped into a pair of rather large shoes—shoes some said were too large for anyone to fill. But fill them he did, usually by

Although this late first-generation Camaro sports a 1970 license plate, the real '70 models were completely restyled.

supplying just what the automobile buyer wanted most. "If vulgarity was called for," that English writer continued, "supreme vulgarity was forthcoming." Yet when elegance and strength of line were called for, Mitchell responded generously. Like the design departments of other automobile companies, GM Styling has had its ugly periods, and GM has built its share of hideous cars. However, the cars from the Mitchell years—the second-generation

Camaro prominent among them—were typically fresh and exciting, often radical, and rarely uninteresting.

During a conversation with Mitchell prior to his retirement, it was suggested that the second-generation Camaro and the 1965-69 Corvair were his two best creations. Mitchell agreed. "The first [1967-69 Camaros] were done too fast, we didn't get a chance to do much," he remembered. "But the second-series cars have been in

production for over a decade now, and they're selling better than ever. . . . Stirling Moss saw the first one and he said, 'Bill, you've really got a classic. The detail, it's not all carved up, it's got a nice sweep.' It's been very popular in Europe, too."

The critical difference that shaped the "1970½" Camaro was the decision that it be a ground-up design. (Actually it was officially a 1970 model, albeit delayed, though popularly referred to as a half-year

edition.) There would be none of the compromises forced on the 1967-69 series, such as a cowl shared with the Nova. "Mitchell had convinced management that the Camaro could stand on its own feet," said one former GM stylist, "that it could be profitable enough to qualify the expense necessary in creating its own unique body dies. Of course, many of the body parts were shared by the Pontiac Firebird." (Firebird would remain basically a Camaro clone, though certain items, notably door panels, would not be interchangeable.)

Unlike the original, the second Camaro design evolved the way it did because the car no longer had to share body parts with a sedan. This gave stylists an unprecedented amount of freedom, though tempered by the increasing number of government standards which often seemed to stifle creativity. What emerged was a shape that could be (and was) successfully updated to

Styling clays for the second-generation Camaro were underway as early as August 1966. A pinched rear deck (*opposite, top*) characterizes this example from September '66. Another study from the same period (*this page, top*) wore an evolution of the '69 Camaro grille. Stylists even compared one of their clays to a Ferrari 275 GTB (*above*).

meet regulations as they took effect, but without the kind of measures that ruined many other cars. For instance, the soft-nose facelift for 1978 made the second-series Camaro look better than ever.

Irv Rybicki, Mitchell's successor and GM vice-president in the early Eighties, remembered the evolution of the 1970½ Camaro in an interview with Michael Lamm: "We started planning [it] immediately after the first project ended. That second car, as I remember, wasn't developed in the studios per se. We initially sat down in what we call the body development room, where we package our vehicles, and we worked very closely with Jack Humbert and Dave Holls; we were in there with [body engineer] Vince Kaptur and we worked every day to get the seat placed just right, the rockers where we wanted them, the cowl at a certain point, always with the mental picture of the silhouette we were after.

"We moved the elements around until we had the package that looked like it would present the kind of body shape we were after—a little shoulder on the car, the wheels right out with the skin, the proper height. . . . I always say to the creative staff in our building that if we can get the anatomy, the shape of the skin is easy. The key to the appearance of a car is in its structure, in its anatomy: where you place the seats, how high, how wide, its length, the correct tumblehome, the proper relationship of the wheels to the sheetmetal. If you've got those elements, you're going to get an automobile that's very appealing to the eye, and that's the way this one was."

The second generation was developed strictly as a coupe. A convertible was never even considered, though a wagon might have come along had there been full body panel interchangeability between Camaro and Firebird. The decision to abandon the convertible came about for two reasons. For one thing, tooling costs would have been considerable because the new F-body would be unrelated to any sedan. This meant tooling would have to be paid for with a much lower production volume—too low to justify a second body style. Also, convertibles had faded in popularity by the end of the Sixties, so potential sales did not justify the expense. The advent of air conditioning and efficient flow-through ventilation systems had contributed to the ragtop's decline.

There was also a fear at the time (unwarranted, as it turned out) that the National Highway Traffic Safety Administration was about to enact standards for rollover protection. Such standards would

Opposite: More second-generation styling studies, from 1966-68. Undated study (*top*) had the split-bumper RS front end, but was a notchback. Semi-fastback styling with rear quarter windows distinguished January '68 study (*second row, right*). *This page:* Front-end concepts offered a variety of treatments for bumper, grille, and headlamps.

have effectively banned the sale of full convertibles in the U.S. Many companies used this as an excuse to drop their open models, but the main reasons were marginal sales and low profitability, not the threat of government regulation.

Once again, the styling brief was placed in the competent hands of Henry Haga. Again, the GM styling hierarchy (including Holls, Rybicki, and Chuck Jordan) observed and directed. Bill Mitchell was still the final authority. But this time, styling compromises were repeatedly shot down. At one point, Rybicki noted, engineers insisted on a higher cowl line than the stylists wanted, so components like heater, radio, glovebox, instrument panel—not to mention the optional air conditioner—would fit. "Hank brought this to my attention, so I met with the engineers," said Rybicki. "But they wouldn't budge. They wanted more space. . . . I called in Bill Mitchell. Bill quickly resolved the situation in a meeting by telling the engineers that a low silhouette was critical to the sporty character of this car, and that we absolutely weren't going to raise the cowl even a fraction of an inch." And that was that.

Was the new model's clean, graceful fastback shape part of the formula from the first? Not really, but it arrived early. Haga and his staff considered many proposals, including notchbacks and semi-fastbacks, with both smoothly rounded and cut-off Kamm-type tails. Some of the initial clay models, done as early as 1966, were reminiscent of the 1968 and later Corvettes. But the near-timeless form that would become familiar to Camaro enthusiasts was simply the one that looked best. And it was never challenged by any committee.

Probably the only serious question about the side elevation was in the greenhouse area: should it have rear quarter windows or not? A variety of treatments were tried. The final solution was to use very long doors and no quarter windows. A few people complained about the size and weight of those doors, but the styling effect was clean and striking. The decision was primarily a matter of cost, according to GM designers. Eliminating that extra piece of glass and its associated hardware freed up money that could be used in other areas of the car.

Front and rear treatments were argued over much longer than the side elevation. Performance-minded stylists wanted a high, aggressive tail with a prominent spoiler, as on the first-generation Z-28s.

This page and opposite: Second-generation Camaro styling studies with suggestions of the final car, though at least one of them took an interesting detour to a novel roof treatment (*this page, bottom*). The November 1967 Prova (*this page, top right*) sported Z-28 badging, dual exhausts, and two-window side styling.

They didn't get it. What prevailed was a smooth, low tail with a semi-Kamm-style flat panel. (Firebird, which was developing at the same time, got a more complex double panel to hide the fact—literally—that its inner trunk wall was shared with Camaro.) Up front, early clays proposed a rather common-looking loop-style bumper surrounding a horizontal-bar grille. This

was scratched in favor of a much more "important-looking" square grille and dual, rather than quad, headlights. The latter choice marked a trend away from the quad setups that had been prevalent in the industry since the late Fifties.

Between headlights and grille, RS models carried smaller round parking lights—a direct crib from the Jaguar XJ sedan, a

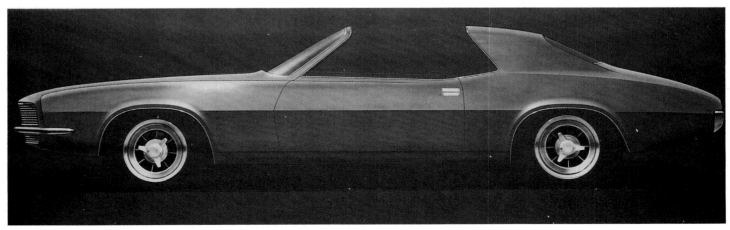

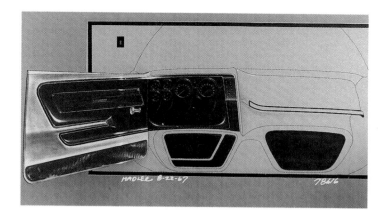

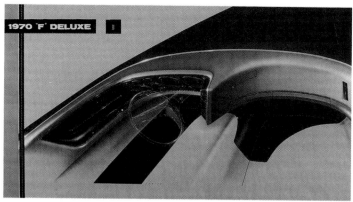

design which had many admirers at GM. An eggcrate grille texture was used to "enrich" the front end far beyond what was normally expected in the car's price class. Instead of a conventional American "face," the new Camaro wore a grille that looked much like those of some very expensive European grand touring cars, notably Ferrari. This helped its lines

enormously, especially compared to the clumsier, more Detroit-style split grille adopted for the Firebird.

The interior was carefully laid out, largely by George Angersbach, in Don Schwarz's studio. Irv Rybicki remained enthusiastic about this aspect of the design: "A lot of time on the interior was spent on 'human engineering.' We were aiming at

something that was close to the Corvette in terms of ride and handling and ease of operation. This had to be a driver's car, with the shift lever correctly placed relative to the steering wheel; all the controls just right.

"For example, if you sit in a Camaro with your hands on the steering wheel, after the seat is properly adjusted, let your

Undated prototypes show near-final Camaro profile and front- and rear-end treatments. Note bumper-exiting exhausts on Prova 70 mockup (*bottom*).

right hand drop off the wheel. It simply falls on the shift knob. The door latch is right where it should be. Every control is equally well placed. The interior is a very good job of human engineering."

With all due respect to Mr. Rybicki, it could be argued that "human engineering" should have been carried further. For instance, the pedals ended up too far forward, requiring long-legged drivers to snug the seat too far up for a comfortable reach to the steering wheel. The wheel itself had a wide horizontal bar that hid the heater controls, turn signal indicators, and ashtray from the driver's sight. The ashtray, in turn, could bang against the driver's knee when pulled out. Federal regulations dictated that the ignition key could not be removed from the column lock without first putting the car in reverse. Instruments were well placed, though, with speedometer and fuel gauge (and optional tachometer) squarely in the middle. However, the tach's "redline" extended from 6500 to 8000 rpm, leaving the driver to wonder exactly what the limit was.

The instrument panel bears mention because it survived unchanged through 1978. Angersbach's design was a variation on the curved panels pioneered in the early Sixties by Pontiac and Studebaker. Unlike these, however, the curved portion of the Camaro's panel did not house the heater controls (mounted below and to the left) or radio (lower right). These items, along with the light and wiper switches, were somewhat awkward to reach.

The general engineering concept of the original Camaro continued on its replacement: unit body/chassis with front sub-frame, a similar lineup of engines, standard front disc brakes. Yet there was a subtle

"deemphasis of performance," as *Sports Car Graphic* magazine put it. For instance, you could no longer order the hairy, roughly idling 302-cid engine (Z-28s now used a 350 V-8). Four-wheel disc brakes were out. Obvious "performance" add-ons like a front air dam or an air-gulping "bubble hood" were also canned. In general, the revised Camaro was more refined, softer, and quieter than the 1967-69 models.

There were two reasons for the changes, as *Sports Car Graphic* noted: "The major one is government [which will probably] drop the guillotine on super cars and factory-installed performance equipment. Since Chevrolet doesn't like to be told what to do, they're getting the jump on our legislators. . . . Reason number two is that performance equipment is expensive, and since SCCA changed its rules regarding availability of options for Trans-Am Championship racing, manufacturers aren't required to produce 'X' number of parts."

With these "givens," here's what Chevrolet engineers did for the 1970½ Camaro. First, the steering linkage was completely redesigned and located ahead of, rather than behind, the front ball joints. Suspension compliance was revised to better deflect road shocks and create final understeer. This made it harder to hang the tail out on the new model than on a '69. (It was still possible, though, if you worked at it.) Out back, multi-leaf rear springs replaced the single-leaf ones, the rear shocks were staggered to reduce rear wheel wind-up, and new spring bushings were developed to prevent lateral shake and body roll. On top of this, Z-28 and SS cars had a special "high-effort" steering gear, which reduced the tendency to over-correct.

A proposal for a two-door Camaro station wagon (*above and bottom*) carried on Chevy's long-standing interest in sporty wagons—similar studies had been done a decade earlier for Corvette. Late coupe prototype (*below*) is very close to finalized version.

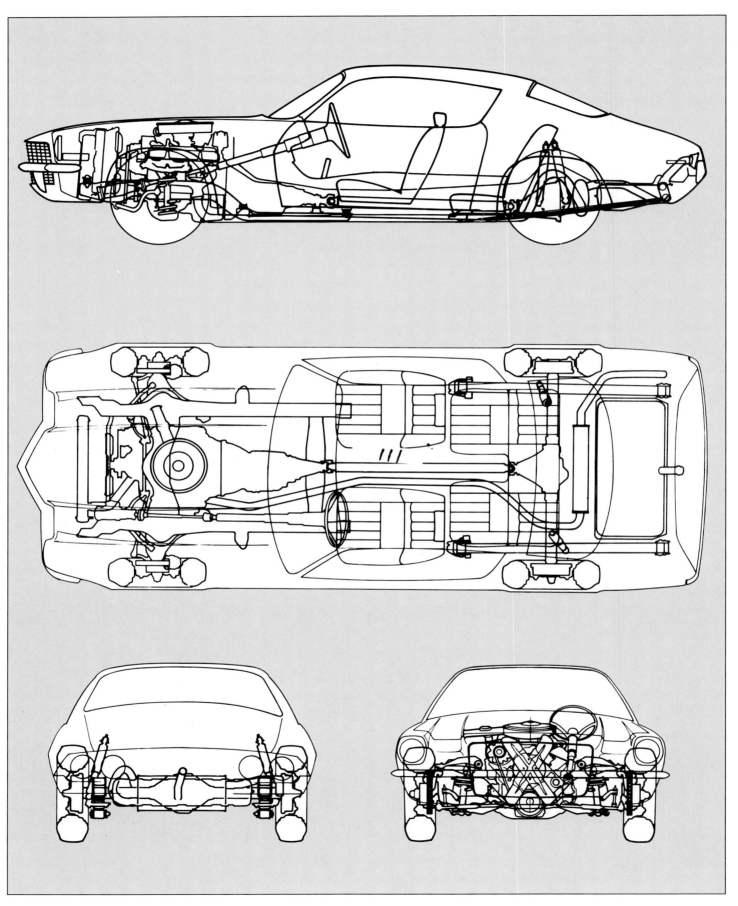

Opposite: GM technical drawings show second-generation Camaro's unit body, front sub-frame, and revised suspension. *This page:* Early publicity shot for the '70 Rally Sport (*above*) clearly emphasizes attributes more subjective than performance. Prototype with ZL-1 badging (*right*) echoed the promise of potent Camaro racers of 1969

The overall result was a supple, forgiving suspension. *Car and Driver* magazine went so far as to pronounce the Camaro's handling "probably the best Detroit has ever produced. The transition as you enter a curve or change is extremely predictable and this, combined with a low body roll angle, is the essence of good road handling." But *C/D* also observed, "In more demanding situations, those which you would encounter on a race track or perhaps on a road you had all to yourself, the Camaro is disappointing. It understeers heavily; sometimes you can trick it and get the tail out, sometimes you just have to slow down until the front tires regain their hold on the pavement." Quite a contradiction within the same paragraph. Most reviewers, however, judged the new suspension one of the best conventional layouts around.

Even more important than the chassis changes was something glossed over by most road testers, though all of them commented on the quietness of the revamped Camaro. Chevrolet had gone through an exhaustive re-engineering process to improve sound isolation in the new body to give it an extremely "tight"

feel. For example, many of the usual welding-access holes through which components are attached during assembly were systematically eliminated. Those that remained were located away from channels and pockets where noise could get through to the interior. Also, there were fewer resonance-sensitive body panels, new sealing at panel joints, reworked side window seals, and a big layer of acoustical material sandwiched between the roof and headliner. These details made the new Camaro body one of the tightest ever produced in Detroit. Total reduction in noise from all sources was 84 percent, against just 28 percent on the 1967-69 Camaro.

Riding the same 108-inch wheelbase as before, the new Camaro was unveiled in late February 1970. Despite the fact that

none of its body panels interchanged with the first generation, its dimensions were little changed—just two inches longer, a tad wider, an inch lower. Of course, the new car was different in many ways, and mostly for the better. For example, overall glass area had been increased 10 percent, despite the lack of quarter windows. About the worst thing you could say of the new design was that the doors were very long and bulky.

The engine lineup was narrower, and there were considerable changes in detail specs. Against 12 offerings for 1969, only seven emerged in 1970. The base six was now the 155-bhp 250-cid unit, the 230 having been banished. Base V-8 was still the 200-bhp 307, with a special 360-bhp 350 V-8 for the Z-28. One 327, two 396s, and the 427 from 1969 were missing.

The '70 Z-28s, seen on these pages in Hugger Orange, boasted a 360-gross-bhp 350 V-8. Z-28 badges were displayed on all four sides. Chevy ad copy touted the '70 Z-28 as made "for the guy who always wanted a performance car that he could drive to work." (Owner: Barry Waddell)

Advertising for 1970 (*above*) emphasized sleek lines; power was provided by optional 350-cid, 360-horsepower V-8 (*top right*). Concise, gently curved dash (*right*) helped fuel buyer enthusiasm. *Sports Car Graphic* declared that the Z-28 (*opposite*) "hasn't lost any of its zing. . . ." (Owner: Stephen F. Collins)

Factory spec sheets listed an eighth powerplant: 454 cubic inches, 450 bhp, and 500 foot-pounds of torque, but this was never actually available. Also, the "396" was really a 402 now, because of a minor bore increase. Chevrolet didn't list it as such because the magic number "396" had earned a following, and the sales people felt it ought to be retained.

With the arrival of the heavier, coupe-only second generation, six-cylinder sales

plummeted. Only after the Arab oil embargo of 1973-74 (and the resultant demand for more economical cars) would six-cylinder Camaros become more popular. Their relative rarity in the early Seventies was due to several factors. First, gasoline was artificially cheap in the U.S., due to government price policy. As a result, most buyers opted for the thirstier V-8s. Second, the all-new 1970½ models were more luxurious than their predecessors.

Exterior and interior options were similar to previous Camaro offerings. Style Trim, RS, SS, and Z-28 packages all continued, and the lineup included two upgraded interiors, "Special" and "Custom." One interesting distinction was that standard (and even Style Trim) models had exposed wipers. To get the optional hidden wipers you had to order the Rally Sport equipment. This also gave a freestanding grille with a urethane-covered frame and split front

bumper, parking lights mounted inboard of the headlights (à la Jaguar XJ), special badges, plus the Style Trim group. As before, the more functional SS equipment could be ordered with or without the RS appearance features. Hardly anyone had specified a bench seat on 1967-69 cars, so buckets were now standard.

Buyers really had to wield the option book to fill up that dashboard. A large speedometer and an equal-size (relatively enormous) fuel gauge were the only standard instruments. Four smaller holes, two on each side of the centrally placed main dials, could hold optional instruments instead of the standard warning lights that looked after all other functions. The gauge package, mandatory for Z-28s, replaced the blanked-off holes with needle instruments for less than $100. The console, too, was optional at $59.

This page and opposite: This '70 Hurst Sunshine Special, a prototype concept car bought from a GM executive, is one of only three built. A 350-cid V-8, prototype auto-stick shifter, and sliding fabric sunroof are highlights. (Owner: Dr. Mike Cruz)

For the most part, the second-generation Camaro was greeted favorably. "A tremendous improvement," was how *Road & Track* magazine saw it. "Puts the Ponycar in a new class." Braking was the big complaint. If anything, brakes were even less fade-resistant than those of earlier models. They were judged adequate for daily use and emergencies, but marginal for vigorous downhill mountain work—a fairly limited criticism. Also, in *R&T's*

opinion, the Camaro was too big for its passenger and cargo capacity. "But overall it's a pleasant, responsive, solid car—very nice to drive in the day-in-day-out routine, and an exceedingly good long-distance touring car. In fact, we'll have to say it's the best American car we've ever driven, and more importantly, it's one of the most satisfying cars for all-around use we've ever driven."

R&T has often tagged various cars as

the best ever driven, so these musings should be taken with the traditional grain of salt. What this evaluation suggested, though, was a very important achievement. After a decade or so of trying, America had finally produced a gran turismo in the true sense of the term: a road car able to carry two passengers and their luggage for long distances in great comfort—rapidly. And thanks to Bill Mitchell's unerring sense of style, it was marvelous to look at.

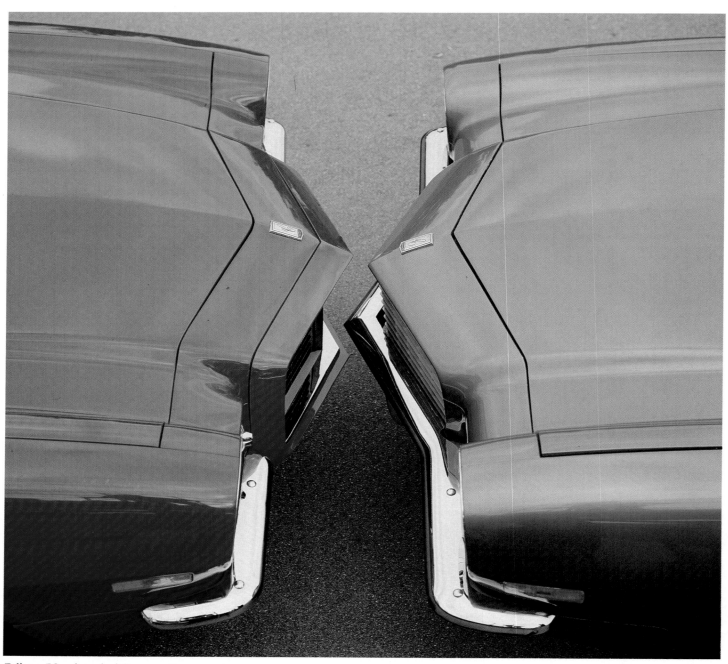

Differing RS and standard-Camaro grilles go nose-to-nose.

The Camaro Model and Engine Lineup for 1970 ½					
Model		**Base Price**	**Weight**	**Production**	
Six-cylinder coupe		$2749	3076	12,566	
V-8 coupe		$2839	3190	112,323	
Engine	**cid**	**bore x stroke**	**bhp @ rpm**	**C.R.**	
Base six	250	3.875 x 3.53	155 @ 4200	8.5:1	
Base V-8	307	3.875 x 3.25	200 @ 4600	9.0:1	
Z-28 V-8	350	4.00 x 3.48	360 @ 6000	11.0:1	
Opt. V-8	350	4.00 x 3.48	250 @ 4800	9.0:1	
Opt. V-8	350	4.00 x 3.48	300 @ 4800	10.25:1	
Opt. V-8	396[1]	4.126 x 3.76	350 @ 5200	10.25:1	
Opt. V-8	396[1]	4.126 x 3.76	375 @ 5600	11.0:1	

Actual displacement was 402 cubic inches, though advertised at 396.

Chapter Four

Camaro in the Seventies: Persistence Pays Off

Camaro came out a winner in the Seventies by fashioning itself into a stylish, roadable, and acceptably quick car that found a secure place in a changing market. In all, it was a distinctly American alternative to imports.

Ponycars were slipping in popularity by the time the all-new 1970½ Camaro arrived. For that reason, GM officials began to consider whether they should continue the line beyond the normal three-year cycle (1970-72). They even wondered whether the plant itself was justified. Camaros and Firebirds were built alongside Novas at Norwood, Ohio, and also at a factory in Van Nuys, California. Given the decrease in ponycar sales, questions were raised about Norwood's long-term viability. Perhaps, some reasoned, it should turn out only Novas.

As it happened, the precarious situation reached a climax in April 1972, when the United Auto Workers union called a strike at Norwood, halting production for almost six months. The union was protesting layoffs that had occurred as F-body sales continued to soften. As a result, Camaro production for the calendar year dropped to 63,832—a record low. After the strike, Nova production was transferred for fear that any further work stoppages at Norwood would hurt the compact's sales, which were still strong. This move further dimmed the F-body's prospects for survival.

What saved the Camaro and Firebird was a determined in-house "public relations" effort by Chevrolet and Pontiac executives, who thought the cars were too good to lose. They argued to GM brass that, even though sales admittedly weren't what they had been, these cars were of strategic importance, especially to dealers. Because they differed so much from rank-and-file Chevy and Pontiac models (except for Corvette), they lured

shoppers into the showrooms. Fortunately, the lobbying campaign worked, and the Camaro/Firebird got a reprieve.

Like many GM decisions, this proved to be a wise move. In time, Mustang evolved into the smaller 1974 Mustang II. Cougar became a specialty offering in the Montego line. Chrysler's Barracuda/Challenger vanished after 1974. AMC's Javelin got controversial styling that led to its demise after 1974. With all these shifts in the competition, GM suddenly found that keeping the Camaro and Firebird around was not only practical, but also positively desirable. Suddenly, these were the only *true* ponycars left. At first, sales didn't pick up, mostly because of the drop in demand for performance cars caused by the 1973-74 oil crisis. But after gas started flowing again, the buyers came back. By 1977, Camaro model year production topped the 200,000 mark, a level it hadn't reached since 1969. In 1978, a record 272,631 cars were built.

But all of this was unknown in 1971-72, when Camaro changed very little—mainly modified just enough to comply with emissions and crash protection laws. You could spot the '71 at a glance by looking at the seats—high-back buckets with built-in headrests taken straight out of the subcompact Vega (the 1970 Camaros had their own low-back seats with separate headrests). Items that were easy and cheap to change (hubcaps, color schemes, upholstery) were shifted, and the Z-28 got a front air dam plus a redesigned rear deck spoiler.

Also beginning in 1971, GM switched

to SAE net horsepower ratings, instead of quoting gross horsepower for its engines. This hardly made the advertising agency's job of promoting the Camaro as a performance car any easier. The 250-cid six was now listed at 110 net horsepower (against 145 gross in 1970). The 402-cid engine (advertised as a 396) rated a lowly 240 bhp net. Many of the performance engines, such as the 350- and 375-bhp 396s, were dropped completely. Cloth-and-vinyl replaced all-vinyl as the standard upholstery material, and the usual assortment of RS and SS appearance and performance packages were carried over.

For 1972—when the crippling Norwood strike made it look like the Camaro's number was up—changes were again minor. Standard models got a facial alteration by the simple measure of reducing the number of vertical bars from 12 to seven, a change that produced larger "eggcrate" holes and a coarser, more aggressive look. The split-grille RS front end was unchanged. Three-point shoulder belts were installed for the first time, at Washington's behest; and during the production run a "fasten seatbelts" warning light was added to the dashboard. New colors were offered for the vinyl roof option, which was now finished in gloss. Interior door panels were markedly changed, and now sported commodious storage compartments. There was even a coin holder under the door handle on the driver's side. Engine power ratings stayed about the same.

Available automatic transmissions of the early Seventies could be controlled by a "stirrup" shifter on the optional console. That console was wide enough to make the front compartment feel a bit tight, but provided a second storage locker. A vertical slot between the fuel gauge and speedometer contained the shift quadrant, while lights and wiper/washer knobs, plus the cigarette lighter, sat at the outer ends of the instrument cluster. The entire dash was finished in textured vinyl, unless the car had the optional Custom Interior (Z87). That also meant vinyl instead of cloth-insert seats; no woodgrain on the instrument panel, console, and door panels; and less insulation in floor, tunnel, and roof areas.

Optional air conditioning, integrated with the powerful heater/defroster, allowed the driver to select almost any climate at a touch of the appropriate lever. Flow-through "Astro Ventilation," with air extractor vents hidden in the door jambs, proved highly effective. Camaro continued to follow ponycar tradition with a back seat that qualified as little more than a temporary perch for adults.

A typical '72 might have a 307-cid V-8, automatic transmission, standard suspension, standard disc/drum brake system, and power steering. This sort of engine/transmission combination could give good low-range acceleration, cruising speed up to about 85 mph, and fuel mileage ranging from 12 to 16 miles per gallon. Out of 68,656 Camaros built during the 1972 model run, nearly 64,000 were V-8s, about 60,000 had power steering, and nearly 58,000 had automatic transmission. Air conditioning was installed in almost half of all Camaros.

Over the road, the typical Camaro of the early Seventies was beautifully smooth, and possessed ample power for passing. Most impressive, at least with a tame drivetrain, might have been its uncanny silence. For a car in its price class, that must have been a revelation, especially compared to the somewhat noisier Mustangs and Cougars. It was no better at carrying four people than they were, but again, that wasn't its main purpose. Some reviewers perpetually bemoaned the lack of rear seat room in ponycars—never mind that a Camaro back seat was rarely used.

Considered as a two-seater, the coupe earned high marks for comfort, and had more than adequate luggage capacity if one counted the back seat as additional cargo room.

The stock suspension was supple and cushy, hardly the underpinnings of a NASCAR champion. Camaro was an understeering car, so it tended to plow a lot in hard corners. But it handled well, if compared to the typical American car of the period rather than to a Z-28 or Shelby-Mustang. Every second-generation Camaro hunkered down low on the road, and gave a ground-hugging appearance from all angles.

As the nation was struck by Camaro fever during the early days of the car's second generation, Chevy responded by creating attention-getting one-offs, like the stunningly beautiful 1970 "Landau" show car (*right and below*) that was built for singer Glen Campbell. The Landau predicted Camaro's T-bar roof option, which arrived much later. For 1972 the Camaro buyer could choose the $306 350 SS package (*opposite*), with 200 net horsepower. A total of 6562 SS models were built in '72. The car seen here also has the desirable $118 split-bumper RS package; 11,364 were ordered.

Despite increasingly fussy federal regulations, Camaro was able to move through the Seventies without radical change. By 1972, promotional photos like the one above were merely implying performance—styling was now the marketing key. Reinforced bumpers satisfied the feds in 1973 (*right*). The '74 Camaro (*opposite*) was pricier than its predecessors, and sported a prow-like nose.

1974

Standard 11-inch front disc and 9.5-inch rear drum brakes were adequate for all but severe driving conditions—going flat-out down Pikes Peak, for instance. Perhaps one driver in a hundred drove hard enough to induce fade. Obviously, anybody ordering power steering, automatic, and air was not too interested in how many fractions of a "g" the car would pull in a tight corner.

New federal bumper-impact regulations arrived for 1973, but Chevy managed to hold onto the Camaro's front end styling without resorting to the "rubber baby buggy bumpers" adopted by some other

car makers. This was done by moving both front and rear bumpers farther away from the body, and reinforcing them with brackets, braces, and an inner support bar.

The trend away from performance was underscored in '73 by the arrival of the Type LT (Luxury Touring) as a replacement for the SS (Super Sport). Ordering an LT delivered a 165-bhp V-8, variable-ratio power steering, and such appearance touches as hidden wipers, black-painted rockers and accents, streamlined "sport" mirrors, Rally wheels, and a woodgrain dashboard. The LT also came with the full set of instruments, deluxe upholstery, and

considerably more insulation than lesser models. Against a base price of $2872 for the standard V-8 coupe, the LT listed at $3268, but the extra $400 bought an appealing selection of goodies.

Prices started to gallop in 1974, with a jump of almost $500 across the board. This year saw the first really serious facelift for the second-generation design. The most notable change was up front, spotlighting a prow-like nose with a beautifully integrated, extruded aluminum-faced bumper. This new ensemble made the car about eight inches longer than the '73. Its design roots may be found in a 1970 show

The Type LT (Luxury Touring) Sport Coupe Camaro arrived for 1973 as a replacement for the Super Sport. The LT's luxury quotient (and price) had increased significantly by 1975 (*above*), and the goodies kept coming for '76 (*opposite*). LT gained a brushed-aluminum rear appliqué and a textured vinyl instrument panel that replaced the woodgrain finish.

car dubbed "Berlinetta" (Italian for "little sedan"), built for Bill Mitchell. Engineering origins date from 1972, when Chevy chose aluminum bars over flat leaf springs as the way to meet the '74 bumper standards. The rear end of the '74 also was altered to accommodate new deeper bumpers and a revised back panel, where smooth, wraparound taillights eliminated the need for the rear side marker beacons.

Overall, these design touches amounted

to extremely deft handling of federal mandates, and eliminated what Bill Mitchell called the "ugly, dirty black bumpers . . . the asphalt stage. . . ." And with a car like the Camaro around, automakers could no longer blame Washington for clumsy "safety car" styling. Clearly, this signaled the beginning of a design renaissance that continued into the Eighties. Detroit had stopped fighting the regulations, and was learning to live with them.

The LT became more luxurious and more costly for '74 (now over $3700 base), and the 307 V-8 was dropped from the engine chart in favor of a detoxed 350 with 145 net horsepower—except in California. This was one year when Californians came out better than buyers in the other 49 states: Their base version of the 350 had a four-barrel carburetor, good for 155 bhp.

The most significant appearance alteration on the 1975 Camaro was a new wraparound rear window, nicely blended into the original greenhouse lines. In fact, the idea had been developed even before the second-generation design was introduced. Sales picked up to the 150,000-unit level again, giving Chevy's ponycar a firm

lease on life. Despite its styling refinements, this was now a five-year-old design — yet it had been so good in the first place that it looked entirely up to date.

Capitalizing on the Camaro's renewed popularity, Chevy revived the Rally Sport package as a splashy mid-season exterior appearance option (RPO Z85), priced at $238. Matte-black paint covered the hood and front fender tops, swept back past the cowl just below the side windows, and then up to cover most of the roof. For the rest of the body, customers had a choice of white, metallic blue, silver, red, or bright canary yellow. When wearing color-matched Z-28 Trans-Am wheels, the new RS was unmistakable.

Also new for '75 were finned rear brake drums, twin-exhaust mufflers on V-8s, High-Energy Ignition for all models, and the first catalytic converter. In addition, Camaros could get a passel of new audio equipment, optional power door locks, and cruise control.

For the first time, too, air conditioning was available on six-cylinder Camaros. By 1974, the number of AC-equipped Camaros had risen to near 80,000, but not with a six. Even after 1975, dealers

commonly urged customers to team AC with a V-8, concerned that "air" would leave the car underpowered with a six. Of course, sixes weren't exactly capturing the hearts of most Camaro buyers anyway. The peak year for six-cylinder Camaros since the onset of the second generation came in 1977, when 38,000 found customers. Yet even that was only 17 percent of the year's total Camaro production.

For 1976-77, the '74 facelift just kept

The two millionth Camaro was produced in May 1978, by which time the '78 base edition (*below*) displayed the eight-year-old body's third and final facelift. Standard engine was the 4.1-liter six with three-speed manual; the optional 5.0-liter V-8 was tweaked via an aluminum intake manifold.

The base '78 (*above*) fitted with the standard six performed more efficiently after picking up the V-8's electronic ignition. The exterior restyle included body-colored front and rear bumpers made of closed-cell plastic. Although Corvette paced the Indy 500 that year, 49 specially trimmed Z-28 Camaros hauled the race queen and other VIPs.

going as Camaro reached, then exceeded, its old sales record of the Sixties. Most styling changes for '76 centered on the popular Type LT. This gained a textured vinyl (instead of woodgrain) instrument panel and a brushed-aluminum rear-panel appliqué. For 1977, the LT offered bright new woven-cloth upholstery instead of the plaid material previously used; vinyl continued as an alternative. Hidden wipers became standard for all models. But the big item was the somewhat surprising return of the Z-28 for 1977½. This new Z-28 was designed around a much different set of priorities than its earlier namesake. Instead of producing a fire-breathing speed machine (which would have been hard to certify in an age of de-smogged

engines and fuel economy standards), Chevy created a true road car.

Another substantial styling shakeup occurred for '78, and the Camaro came out looking even more like Mitchell's Berlinetta show car. The reworked nose carried grillework above and below a faired-in, body-color bumper. Out back were wider, tri-color taillamps set against a black or silver rear-end panel. There were new interiors and new colors inside and out. A milestone was marked when Camaro number two million was produced on May 11, 1978.

Although a wide range of options was offered, the engine lineup was not nearly as broad as it once had been, and prices stood a lot higher:

	Six	V-8
Sport coupe	$4414	$4599
Rally Sport	4784	4965
LT	4814	4999
LT Rally Sport	5065	5250
Z-28	—	5604

The Style Trim package continued as a $70 option for all models.

LT became "Berlinetta" for 1979, as GM finally adopted the name that had graced various Ferraris, the Camaro show car, and a European Opel Manta model. (GM photographs reveal the name had been considered for an option package proposed for the late-'69 first-generation cars.) The main styling change occurred inside, where the concave-oval instrument panel was finally revised—the old dies had simply worn out! Its replacement retained the same basic layout and instrument location, but had a wider, squarer upper portion that incorporated ventilation outlets plus lights and wiper/washer switches. Heater controls and the radio still sat below the main cluster.

For 1980, the same basic confection was back again. Camaro was now pretty thirsty compared to most other GM cars, but as popular as ever. Four versions were cataloged: standard coupe, RS, Berlinetta, and Z-28, with base prices ranging from $5499 to $7121. Standard this year was a smaller, Chevy-built 229-cid V-6 with 110 bhp, replacing the less thrifty 250-inline six.

The Berlinetta—introduced in 1979 (*above*) to replace the LT—was the ultimate expression of Camaro cushiness and gadgetry. Thanks in part to canny marketing, the car was well-received by buyers. Chevy ad writers described the Berlinetta as "A new way to take your pulse . . . a superb balance between the qualities of a sporty road car and the comfort of a fine touring car."

This new engine, available in all models save the Z-28, gave its best performance when mated with the four-speed manual transmission—although it was no powerhouse to begin with. For *real* performance, there was still no choice but the Z-28. And despite everything that had been legislated to discourage such cars, this Camaro would still turn 0-60 mph times of less than 10 seconds—quite a feat for a federally approved 1980 car.

The second-generation design made its 11th and final bow for the 1981 model year. Though the basic package was altered only in detail, Chevrolet did its best to make the valedictory edition the nicest of this long line.

The elimination of the Rally Sport variant—really just a "cosmetic performance" car in later years—left three models for '81. Base power for the standard but well-equipped Sport Coupe and the even better-equipped Berlinetta was provided by Chevy's 229-cid V-6. Though its 110 bhp wasn't much to move a 3400-pound car around very quickly, it would deliver reasonable gas mileage, especially when teamed with the new four-speed manual gearbox. This $133 option gave much better through-the-gears flexibility than the standard three-speeder, and was much more fun, making its low price seem like peanuts. Minor mechanical improvements included adoption of low-drag calipers for the front disc brakes; a low-effort hydraulic brake booster became standard equipment for all models.

In line with gasoline engines at other GM divisions in 1981, all Camaro power units were treated to the company's newly developed Computer Command Control (CCC) electronic engine management/emissions control system. Besides cleaning up the exhaust, CCC also governed engagement of the lockup torque converter clutch on the extra-cost three-speed automatic transmission. The lockup clutch virtually eliminated fuel-wasting converter slip by providing direct mechanical linkage between the flywheel and the propshaft in third gear, once a preset road speed (about 40 mph) was reached. It was another "subtle extreme" to enhance the mileage potential of what had become—according to changing standards of the day—a heavy, thirsty car.

No-extra-cost standard equipment for the Sport Coupe expanded for '81 to include steel-belted radial tires, twin "sport" door mirrors (the left one adjustable from inside), center console, four-spoke steering wheel, color-keyed cut-pile carpeting,

power steering and brakes, and a big 21-gallon fuel tank. A relatively modest $800 extra bought the swanky Berlinetta. Here, Chevy went all out in quest of refinement by making its Quiet Sound Group standard. This comprised an inner sound-absorbing roof layer, bottom door seals, and an inside roof covering made of soft foam-backed material. The rest of the standard Berlinetta fare included the Custom Trim Group (carpeted lower door

panels and soft, contoured bucket seats); special courtesy light package; and complete instrumentation, from voltmeter to tachometer. Outside were special pinstriping and paint treatment, whitewall tires, and wire wheel covers. A new option was a wheel-cover locking package for theft protection.

Of course, the burly Z-28 was still around, but its big 350 V-8 was now an extra, and Turbo Hydra-matic transmission

This page and opposite: At $7576, the '81 Berlinetta was priced midway between the Sport Coupe and the Z-28. Standard features besides the 3.8-liter V-6 included a bright-accented argent grille, Quiet Sound Group, specific badging, and special striping on the bumpers and lower bodysides; the striping could be had in black, silver, gold, red, blue, or beige. The options list was long, so buyers could customize their Camaros to suit their own tastes. Note, for example, the different wheels on the pair of Berlinettas seen on these pages.

CAMARO SECOND-GENERATION MODEL YEAR PRODUCTION, 1971-81

Year	Z-28	Other V-8	Six	Total
1971	4862	98,590	11,191	114,643
1972	2575	61,257	4824	68,656
1973	11,574	81,564	3618	96,756
1974	13,802	115,008	22,198	151,008
1975	—	116,430	29,359	145,789
1976	—	144,934	38,047	182,981
1977	14,349	173,115	31,390	218,854
1978	54,907	180,742	36,982	272,631
1979	84,879	175,779	21,913	282,571
1980	45,143	55,758	51,104	152,005
1981	43,272	30,863	52,004	126,139

was mandatory. After a one-year absence, the 350 was again certified for California.

Between the base V-6 and the Z's V-8s was an intermediate 267-cid V-8, optional for Sport Coupe and Berlinetta only (but not in California). Golden State buyers who preferred the base powerplant got a Buick-built 231-cid unit, not the Chevy 229, although rated at the same 110 bhp. Even though Detroit had been coping with emissions standards for over 10 years, it still found drivetrain gyrations of this sort a necessity to meet California's ever-stiffer requirements.

The '81 model served as a fitting finale for the enduring second-generation Camaro. To quote that year's brochure (which, with its Art Deco cover, is nearly as much of a collector's item as the car itself), the last of this hardy breed was "sleek and crisp [with]

showstopping good looks, unmistakable zest for hugging the road and capturing the heart, and a flair for moving through life with style."

The second generation certainly maintained its style—and a good deal of its performance—as it moved through its long production life. Even after 11 years, Camaro still looked great, and remained one of the quickest cars in a land increasingly populated by four-cylinder econoboxes and "paint-on performance" cars. Its basic shape, on the drawing board as early as 1968, had defiantly stood the test of time. And Camaro defied conventional wisdom by gaining increased sales in the face of government regulations, inflation, fuel shortages and price hikes, serious challenges from sporty imports, and Detroit's growing preoccupation with downsizing

in the Seventies.

Camaro's exterior lines seemed "just right." Though vinyl tops were popular add-ons in these years, the car's unadorned shape was so pure that it somehow seemed wrong to break up those lines with a vinyl roof.

Critics may argue that the second-generation Camaro was allowed to hang on too long, that it had become woefully outmoded in the radically changed automotive world of the early Eighties. True enough, but such carping misses the point: The original 1970 design not only aged gracefully, but actually got better with each passing year. Maybe that's why this series remained so popular right up to the end. Without a doubt, these Camaros will enjoy a secure place in the hearts and minds of enthusiasts for years to come.

Simulated wire wheels (*opposite*) were one tip-off that the 1981 Berlinetta was the luxury Camaro. Inside, a four-spoke steering wheel with a Berlinetta nameplate highlighted the plush interior (*above*). The 110 horsepower created by the '81 Berlinetta's standard V-6 wasn't sufficient to move a 3400-pound car around very quickly, but it did deliver reasonable gas mileage. (Owner: Debra L. Hogan)

Camaro engines (displacement/net horsepower) 1971-81

	1971	1972	1973	1974	1975	1976	1977	1978	1979	1980	1981
Base six, cid	250	250	250	250	250	250	250	250	250	229	229
bhp	110	110	100	100	105	105	110[1]	110[1]	115[1]	115[5]	110[5]
Base V-8, cid	307	307	307	350	350	305	305	305	305	267	267
bhp	140	130	115	145[2]	145[2]	140	145	145	130	120	190
Z-28/V-8, cid	350	350	350	350			350	350	350	350[6]	350
bhp	275	255	245	245			185[3]	185[3]	175[4]	190	175
Opt. V-8, cid	350	350	350	350	350	350	350	350	350	305	305
bhp	165	165	145	185	155	165	170	170	170	155	165
Opt. V-8, cid	350	350	350								
bhp	210	200	175								
Opt. V-8, cid	402	402									
bhp	260	240									
Cal. V-8, cid				350	350		305	305	305		
bhp				160	155		135	135	135		
Cal. V-8, cid							350	350	350		
bhp							160	160	165		

1 = 90-bhp in California; 2 = n.a. California; 3 = 175-bhp Cal. or hi-altitude; 4 = 170-bhp California or hi-altitude; 5 = 110-bhp 231-cid V-6 California; 6 = 165-bhp, 305-cid V-8 California.

Chapter Five

Rebirth of the Z: Just a Little Less Substance

Revived in mid-year 1977 after a two-year hiatus, the Z-28s of the late Seventies were a breed very different from their predecessors of either the first or second generation. The second-generation cars split evenly into two groups: 1970-74 and 1977-81. No Z-28s at all were produced in the interim period.

The 1970 edition received a new powerplant: a smooth 360-horsepower version of the 350-cid V-8, derived from the Corvette LT1 unit. This engine used a forged-steel crankshaft and four-bolt main bearings. Fuel entered a Holley four-barrel carburetor fitted to an aluminum high-rise manifold. Mechanical valve lifters, heads from the 302 engine, a chrome dress-up kit, and high-capacity radiator were all standard. The chassis was essentially unchanged from 1969, though a thicker front anti-roll bar was used. Some 1970 models can be distinguished by their low-profile rear spoilers, similar to the 1967-69 design, which was phased out after 1971 in favor of the taller integrated version that continued through 1981.

In performance, the '70 was every bit as hot as its forerunners—some said even hotter. Yet this was not the roughly-idling machine the '69 was—far from it. The new Z-28 was marked by turbine-like smoothness, mainly because the 350 was not a thinly disguised racing engine, like the 302. Rather, it was designed with an eye to the government's emission limits, which would become more and more exacting over the next several years.

Widening governmental influence on car design was seen in the Z-28 for 1971. That year the industry responded to critics of the "horsepower race" by advertising engine output in SAE net (rather than gross) figures—which gave a more realistic appraisal of actual power available. GM also adopted a self-imposed limit on compression ratios (no higher than 8.5:1), so its cars would run on leaded or low-lead regular gas. The Z-28, Pontiac Trans Am, and Corvette were exempt, however, and used 9:1 compression. Even so, the horse-power of the Camaro's 350 V-8 came in at 330 gross (275 net), down from 360 in 1970.

Through 1974, horsepower ratings kept sliding as emission controls began strangling performance engines. Net power fell to 255 bhp for 1972, then slipped to 245 for 1973-74. Very few engine modifications were made during this time, except for the addition of hydraulic lifters in 1972. The steering ratio, which had varied often, now stayed at 16:1, with power assist mandatory. Powerglide left the lineup, making Turbo Hydra-matic the sole transmission option.

By de-emphasizing the performance aspects of the Z-28, Chevy was eventually able to reduce the cost of the package. The option sold for nearly $800 in 1971; by 1973 it was down to $500. Contributing to the cut was the decision to drop the expensive high-rise aluminum manifold after 1972. Another sign that things weren't quite what they used to be was the disappearance of the "drag-strip" 4.10:1 rear axle ratio in 1973. Also in that year, Positraction became a standard item, and the first Z-cars with air conditioning were produced.

Very little changed for the 1974 edition, although "High-Energy" solid-state ignition came along at mid-year. Mechanical differences were limited to making power steering a standard Z item, and the use of aluminum cases for all four-speed transmissions. The '74s were decorated with bright new hood and rear deck graphics, and had black-painted grillework outlined in silver.

In 1974, one GM executive explained, the company had decided to "kill the car before it died a slow, lingering death." The Arab oil embargo, which created block-long waiting lines at every gas-short service station, suddenly rendered the Z-28 almost unsalable. Even after Camaro sales as a whole began recovering toward the end of the model year, GM was reluctant to continue the Z-car. It would have to overcome the strictest emissions limits yet, and also meet new noise standards. The expense of bringing the car into compliance seemed just too great in view of its questionable sales potential. Thus, the Z-28 was abruptly and unceremoniously dropped.

Why then was it brought back in mid-1977? The return was essentially a marketing decision, though thousands of enthusiasts applauded its debut at the Chicago Auto Show, with a $5170 price tag. During 1974 and 1975, Camaros had returned to the competition lists, running with distinction in the International Race of Champions (IROC) in the hands of its old friends at Penske Racing. With this kind of publicity spin-off, it made sense to return the Z-28 to the showrooms. Cleverly, however, GM did not pick up where it had left off and build a street version of a racer. Instead, the production Z was revived as a grand tourer, able to hold its own with the best from Europe. Though the focus was now clearly on handling, Chevy engineers gave it as much get-up-and-go as they possibly could, given the state of emissions technology in the late '70s.

Suspension engineering for the new Z-28 was handled by Jack W. Turner, Jr. His approach was straightforward: tighter springs at each corner, a thicker anti-roll bar up front, and a more flexible rear bar combined with larger wheels and tires.

"We had a number of ways to go," Turner explained. "We could put roll stiffness into the vehicle with just stabilizer bars, but then it's not too good on tramp input. . . . We tried to pick a happy medium between going up in spring rates and still not having to add humongous stabilizer bars. We tried to balance the system so the car could go over road undulations and go into corners with chatter bumps so that the suspension would allow the tires to envelope some of that roughness. . . . That means a lot of refinement between the shock valving, spring rate, and stabilizer bar rate."

Turner also gave the car faster steering, with a 13.02:1 ratio compared to 14.3:1

The Z-28 was in deadly peril for the
first half of the Seventies; indeed, the
car disappeared for two years at
mid-decade. But the Z-28 would return.

The Z-28 was a $598 package option in 1973. As before, the
350 V-8 provided the power, though it was down 10 bhp from
'72, to 245. (Owner: Kurt A. Gardner)

For 1973 (*this page and opposite*), the Z-28 could be ordered with air conditioning, a new option. The hydraulic-lifter V-8 (*right*) was no weak sister, but the powerplant was definitely hobbled by emissions controls. *Motor Trend* timed a '73 Z-28 with automatic transmission at a sluggish 10 seconds in the 0-60 sprint. Top speed was 110, down from the 1970 Z-28's 130. (Owner: Kurt A. Gardner)

on the '74. Wheels were 15 × 7 inches, carrying Goodyear GR7015 steel-belted radial tires. Under the hood sat the relatively tame, 185-bhp (net) version of the 350-cid V8, breathing through a four-barrel Rochester carburetor. The four-bolt mains, forged crank, and long-duration cam of past Z-cars were nowhere to be found.

The 1978-81 Z-28 was essentially just an evolution of the 1977½ package, starting with an aggressively facelifted '78 that built upon Camaro's new soft front/rear fascia and tri-color taillamps. Advertising promised that the hottest Camaro, wearing revised striping, spoiler, and fender louvers, would "put butterflies in your stomach, a lump in your throat and a smile on your face." The '79 edition had fewer horses and new graphics, a wraparound front air

dam, and a new instrument panel shared with other Camaros that year.

Like other Camaros, the Z-28 of the late Seventies had big doors that opened onto large, comfortable bucket seats. Even the rear seat seemed deeper and more "buckety" than earlier editions, though road-testers generally described it as a bench. (For 1979, the back seat actually was separated by eliminating the thinly padded connecting portion over the driveshaft tunnel.) The smallish steering wheel wore simulated string wrapping on the rim, for a tighter grip, though its four spokes tended to obscure the full array of instruments, which were otherwise very legible.

In spite of the fact that late-Seventies Zs were known primarily as "driver's cars," they were no slouches at straight-line

performance. Blasting from a standing start to 60 mph took as little as 7.5 seconds—near Sixties hot-rod capability, and hardly what you'd expect in a car of this vintage. Of course, leadfooted driving returned single-digit mpg figures, which didn't exactly endear this car to conservationists. With so much torque available, even a mild-mannered person behind the wheel of a manual-shift Camaro could easily drive off in first and shift directly to fourth once the car got rolling.

Give the Z-28 its head on some fast turns, and you'd get proof positive of how well the suspension engineers did their work. Simply put, the car stuck to the road like glue. A slight plowing tendency became apparent only in extremely tight corners. On a bend at 50 mph or better, the beast would just dig in and keep gain-

ing momentum. Tracking and stability on superhighways registered as virtually faultless.

Even bolder styling for 1980's "Maximum Camaro" included a rear-facing hood scoop that sucked in cold air under full throttle, plus fender vents that released hot engine air. These changes weren't enough to keep sales strong in the wake of the nation's second oil crunch of the decade. In 1981, for the first time in several seasons, performance fans could again get a four-speed in a Z-28, though they had to settle for the smaller standard engine, a 305-cid V-8 with four-barrel carb. With automatic and either Z-28 engine, the lockup con-

verter clutch was effective in second gear as well as third.

Considering that the Z-28 would still deliver Sixties-style acceleration and top speed, its $8300 base price in 1981 was rather reasonable in an inflation-ridden market. For those who could afford the gas, it delivered the kind of driving thrill found in few other American cars, with the notable exception of its Corvette brother and Pontiac Firebird Trans Am cousin. And it was still a wild-looking machine, with a deep front air dam, graceful rear spoiler, colorful tape graphics, wheel opening flares, hood scoop with decal, raised-white-letter tires, and body-

Though it still ran with the detoxed 245-bhp 350 V-8, the '74 Z-28 (*above*) made a bold visual statement. Despite the fact that 13,802 Z-28s were built for '74, the car disappeared from the Camaro lineup after the model run. Happily, the Z-28 returned in mid-1977. This GM publicity photo (*opposite*) displays many of the "1977½" Z-28's components, including the 350 V-8, specific manual and automatic transmissions and axles, and suspension system. Suggested retail price was $5170.

This page and opposite: The reformulated 1977½ Z-28 bowed at the Chicago Auto Show in February of that year. Rated at 60 horsepower less than the 1974 model, it was now promoted as a more balanced car. Regardless, it still strutted "boy-racer" stripes, front and rear spoilers, and sporty wheels. *Motor Trend*'s test driver called it "The best handling American production car I've ever driven." The dash (*right*) boasted full instrumentation. (Owner: Richard Matzer)

80

Opposite: Horsepower on the resurrected '77½ Z-28 was 185; 175 for California. Production came to 14,349 units. By 1978 (*this page*), the Z-28 listed at $5604, some $400 more than in '77. The aggressive exterior embellishment continued, and was at least partially justified by many heavy-duty components.

color sport wheels. Just for the record, CONSUMER GUIDE® magazine's testers sprinted from 0 to 60 mph in a brisk 9.2 seconds with a 350/automatic Z-28.

Practical considerations like rear seat legroom, visibility, and trunk space seem almost secondary in a car of this caliber, but they ought to be mentioned. To be honest, no Camaro ever had much room in the back. Though stylish, the somewhat broad rear roof pillars tended to make life difficult when the driver tried to angle into a tight parking space. The trunk amounted to little more than a "Lilliputian foot locker," as one observer put it, so owners learned to dump most of their travel gear in the back seat.

In regular CONSUMER GUIDE® magazine test reports, aimed at ordinary car

Another price jump was in the works for the 1979 Z-28 (*opposite*), to $6748. Distinguishing features included sporty alloy wheels, specific bodyside striping and lettering, and front fendervents. (Owner: Michael Rooney) Z-28 appearance became even splashier for 1980 (*this page, top*) and '81 (*above*).

buyers, the revived Z-28s earned rather low ratings. Enthusiast publications tended to be somewhat less critical, praising the Z-28's virtues and winking at its vices.

What the Z-car fan has always wanted most are style and performance—and the car delivered these in abundance. Bold graphics and aggressive details—Rally wheels, prominent spoiler, black-out grille—gave it the requisite muscular personality. As a comfortable, high-speed, two-passenger GT, the Z-28 ranks among the very best this country has produced.

Nevertheless, this car's sensations belong to a bygone world. Just imagine: Nestled in the dark confines of the cockpit, you stare eagerly at the 130-mph speedometer. Grab the big, clunky shift lever, floor the throttle—instantly, you'd find yourself pinned to the big bucket seat by the

accelerative G-forces as the car squats down and rockets away to become a tiny dot on the horizon. Such were the joys of yesteryear, when just about every kid wanted this sort of car.

After 1981, Camaros of this unabashed nature departed Chevy showrooms and the 1967-81 Zs took on the status of retired champions, driven by a relative handful of enthusiasts. Many believed the Z-28 concept couldn't survive in the toned-down world of the Eighties, but the name entered a new life in the next generation of Camaros. It remains very much alive in the Nineties, as we shall see in the next chapters.

Chapter Six

Generation Three: New Beginnings

As the Camaro closed out its second generation in 1981, the pundits proclaimed, "Performance cars are dead." As with Mark Twain's ironic complaint a century earlier, when a newspaper had published his obituary while he was quite alive, the hand-wringing dirges proved to be premature. Oh yes, the new Camaro would be different, a giant step removed from some of the hairy-chested, throbbing-exhaust beasties that had taken the name a few years previously. But dead? Not just yet, thank you. Chevrolet was prepared to help spark a revival of the performance market with its restyled Camaro, not preside over its demise.

Once in a while, in fact, good cars stretch toward greatness—even if the process takes a long while. For only the third time in 15 years, Chevrolet's ponycar was completely redesigned for 1982. It wasn't an easy job. Originally slated for 1980 introduction, the new Camaro (and its Pontiac Firebird companion, developed alongside) had one of the lengthiest gestation periods in GM history, nearly seven years.

There were reasons, of course, starting with the surprising longevity of the second generation. In mid-1975, when initial work on the 1980 F-car program began, the "old" design had been given the first of two facelifts. Sales were just beginning to recover from their 1972-73 low, which, at one point, nearly spelled the end for Camaro and Firebird. Sales then took off, setting new records each year. This was due in part to GM's ability to update the cars, successfully retaining their excitement and enthusiast appeal in an age when most Detroit products were growing progressively duller. This surprising sales strength must have suggested to GM product planners that any replacement shouldn't deviate too much from the winning formula.

Nevertheless, the second generation's basic engineering was aging even at mid-decade, and would seem more outmoded with each passing year. Clearly a successor would eventually be needed, though no one knew precisely when. For many

By early 1981, Camaro was being outsold by Mustang by a five-to-three margin. The second-generation Camaro had grown old, but invigorating change was in the air.

within GM, creating it was a matter of pride. A new Camaro would have to be as good as GM could make it: sleeker and more aerodynamic, better-handling, more economical, more practical. How else to follow a winner?

By the mid-Seventies, GM was firmly committed to downsizing its entire fleet in order to meet federally mandated corporate average fuel economy (CAFE) requirements that would take effect with the 1978 model year. Thus, there was never any question that the third-generation Camaro/Firebird would have to be smaller and lighter.

One vital question had to be answered first: Should the new models have front- or rear-wheel drive? Each layout had its advocates among GM designers, engineers, product planners—even the company's top officials. For a time, front drive was favored, particularly by the production cost counters, who liked the idea of shared components between a new F-car and the redesigned FWD X-body compacts and/or the later J-car subcompacts. Others, notably Chevrolet chief vehicles engineer Tom Zimmer, were convinced that only rear drive would enable the new Camaro to maintain or better the handling/road-holding ability that had accounted for a large part of the second generation's popularity. A series of top-echelon personnel changes in these years only added to the indecision and delay.

Ultimately, GM's powerful Product Policy Group endorsed rear drive. Less than 11 months later, in December 1978, the production-ready third-generation design got the corporate nod.

General styling inspiration for the new F-cars came from a clay scale model created in October 1976 by Roger Hughet, then an assistant to Advanced One studio

Roger Hughet, then assistant to Advanced One styling studio director William L. Porter, created a clay scale model in October 1976 that suggested the shape of the third-generation Camaro. Hughet's color sketch (*below*) followed.

Chevy designers wanted to be sure that the third-generation Camaro remained recognizably a Camaro. This rough sketch by Chevy design chief Jerry Palmer (*above*) suggests the blend of the familiar and the new that came together on the '82 Camaro (*opposite*).

director William L. Porter (formerly head of Pontiac styling). The most striking feature of Hughet's smooth, flowing model was its roof: a dome made entirely of glass with concealed support pillars. Though this proposal had envisioned front drive, it was "rescued" by David R. Holls, then director for all of GM's advanced design groups, after the decision had been made to stay with rear drive. It quickly became the "theme" model for the eventual '82 F-cars.

"Productionizing" this basic shape was handed over to two teams. Both worked under the direction of Irwin W. Rybicki, who had succeeded William L. Mitchell as GM's Vice-President for Design in August 1977. Rybicki immediately got involved with the program, dictating the use of one-piece side glass (as on the second generation) and crisper, tighter lines. The new Camaro took shape at Chevrolet Studio Three under Jerry Palmer, who would go on to create the stunning 1984 Corvette. A parallel Firebird group was set up at Pontiac Studio Two, supervised by John Schinella. Meanwhile, Camaro engineering was proceeding, largely under Zimmer, but with important contributions from handling group director Fred Schaafsma and Chevrolet chief chassis engineer Robert J. Haglund.

What emerged from all these efforts was

well worth the wait: The '82 Camaro was, simply, a knockout. Despite its smaller external size, Palmer astutely retained recognizable Camaro elements (tri-color taillamps, exposed headlamps, gaping "mouth" grille), but wrapped them in a handsomely different shape—clean, rakish, and just a little intimidating. The influence of Hughet's theme model was seen in a complex, compound-curve backlight, shared with Firebird and said to be the most intricate and costly piece of glass-making ever found in a production car. Lifting up hatch-fashion, it provided more convenient access to the luggage space than the second generation's tiny trunklid. As a bonus, the rear seatback could fold down to provide extra cargo room. A 62-degree slant to the windshield and an impressive 0.368 drag coefficient helped the car slice through the air.

The bodyshell was still wide, lending an air of spaciousness to the interior. A brand-new, high-tech, black-finished dash dominated the cabin, which was planned around a standard center console on all models. Full instrumentation was included on the luxury Berlinetta and high-performance Z28. (By now, that designation was printed without a hyphen in Chevrolet literature and in many, but not all, other sources.) Six-way power seats became a first-time Camaro option, and a new extra-

cost "Conteur" driver's seat from Lear-Siegler boasted lumbar and thigh support adjusters similar to those of the well-known Recaro buckets. Each of the three models displayed its own styling touches, including front air dams and rear fascia, with the Z28's "ground effects" elements hugging the pavement. Specific Z28 gear also included P215/65R15 white-letter tires on five-spoke aluminum wheels with gold or charcoal accents, plus dual air scoops on the hood.

Overall length for the '82 Camaro was cut a substantial 18 inches, with wheelbase pared from 108 to 101 inches. Despite the loss of an average 470 pounds from the '81 models, curb weight was still fairly high—close to 3200 pounds for the Z28, the heavyweight of the three-model lineup. The reason for this was the need for exceptional rigidity in the unit body/chassis structure to resist flexing in suspension, steering, and body, which could impair

handling. To accomplish that, and to save some weight, engineers eliminated the F-car's traditional front subframe, so major drivetrain and suspension components bolted directly to the main structure.

Major revisions hit the suspension itself. The front switched from the familiar upper-and-lower A-arm arrangement to a more compact MacPherson strut/lower control arm layout, still with coil springs. The rear axle remained solid, but was now suspended on coil instead of leaf springs. It was more securely located, too, via a longitudinal torque tube and control arms running ahead of the axle, plus a lateral track bar (Panhard rod).

Significantly, the Z28 chassis was engineered first, mainly because Zimmer and Schaafsma wanted the new Camaro to offer the ultimate in handling. Chassis tuning for lesser models was determined afterward, not the other way around as in former years. Zimmer's own handling target was high: 0.9g lateral acceleration. As it turned out, the production Z28 wasn't far off the mark, recording an impressive 0.839 at the GM Proving Grounds.

Equally significant was the decision to retain V-8 engines for both Camaro and Firebird. Though many GM executives no doubt lobbied for it, the main impetus probably came from F. James McDonald,

vice president for North American automotive operations in the program's later phases and later GM president. McDonald felt this was a "must" to ensure success for the new models and, in particular, to uphold the strong performance image established by the Z28 and Trans Am in the Seventies.

Even so, a revolutionary change took shape under the new Camaro's hood. For the first time, the standard powerplant was a four; specifically, the Pontiac-built 2.5-liter (151-cid) inline unit known as the "Iron Duke," which saw progressively wider application at GM in the late Seventies and early Eighties. For 1982, it

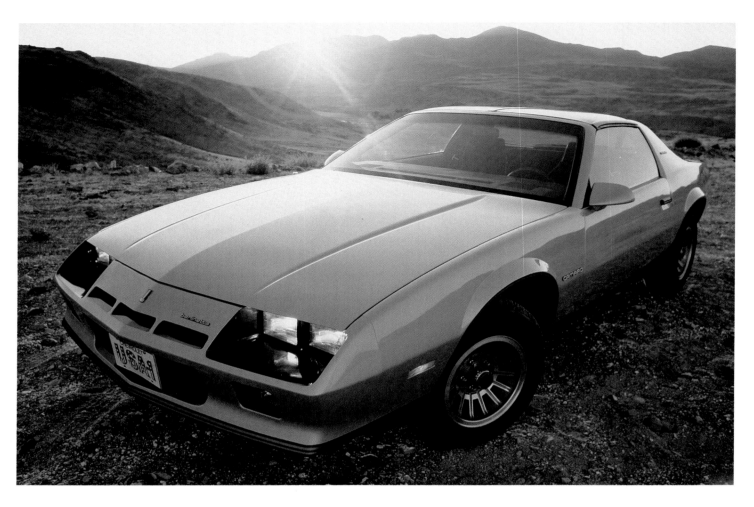

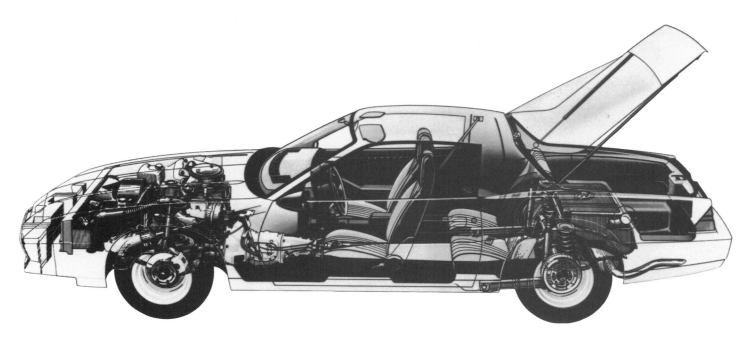

Every observer was struck by the '82 Camaro's compound-curve backlight, a costly and intricate piece of workmanship that lifted up hatch-fashion. The rest of the car was a beaut, too, whether in Berlinetta (*opposite, top*) or Z28 guise (*opposite, bottom*). The '83 Z28 (*above*) rolled with a McPherson Strut front suspension, coil spring rear suspension, and a fuel tank tucked above the rear axle. Camaro's first-ever five-speed manual was also offered in '83.

gained the company's newly developed, carburetor-like throttle-body fuel injection system with electronic control. Standard on the base Sport Coupe, this engine was a credit option for Berlinetta, which was otherwise equipped with Chevy's fine 60-degree 2.8-liter (173-cid) V-6, first seen in the front-drive X-car compacts. In the Camaro, of course, it was mounted north-south instead of transversely, with different horsepower/torque ratings.

The Z28 was finally shorn of its old 350-cid V-8 in favor of the smaller 5.0-liter (305-cid) unit, with four-barrel carb, also optional on other Camaros. The hottest Camaro engine was a fuel-injected version of the small-block, available only for the Z28 with a $450 price tag, featuring the "Cross Fire" ram induction system developed for the '82 Corvette. A total of 24,673 CFI V-8s went under '82 hoods. There was another "first," too: Camaro and Firebird drivetrain offerings were now completely identical. Because a four-speed manual shift was now standard in the Sport Coupe, the old three-speed gearshift became extinct.

Together with Firebird, the new Camaro was one of the few bright spots for GM in a mostly depressed 1982 market—proof that styling could still move cars out of the showrooms, even in an age of tight money and soaring interest rates. Camaro was quickly acclaimed Car of the Year by *Motor Trend* magazine, and the Z28 was chosen as pace car for the 1982 Indy 500. Chevy promptly cranked out 6360 "Commemorative Edition" pace car replicas with the Cross-Fire V-8 and automatic. Though mechanically identical to the normal Z28, these boasted a fancier interior, special blue and silver color scheme (with red accents), and prominent pace car decals.

CONSUMER GUIDE® magazine's editors termed the '82 Camaro an improvement in most respects over its predecessors. Criticisms included the beefy, high-effort manual-shift linkage and the low-slung driving position that hindered outward visibility. On the plus side: taut handling and crisp steering, the extra practicality of the new hatchback feature, the racy-looking dash, and the sexy new shape.

Could it perform? Well, *Road & Track* managed to accelerate to 60 mph in 9.7 seconds and run the quarter-mile in 17.5, in a Z28 with the 145-bhp base engine. Not exactly a record-setting pace, but more than respectable for the period.

In this inflationary era, it was no surprise that the new model cost more. Base prices at the time of the car's January 1982 debut were $976 to $1810 higher than 1981 equivalents, ranging from $7631 for a four-cylinder Sport Coupe to $9700 for the Z28.

Chevrolet advertising downplayed the

An '82 Camaro paced that year's Indianapolis 500. Publicity breeds production, and Chevy offered 6360 replicas to the public.

For 1983, a high-output (H.O.) 305 V-8 with a four-barrel carb (*above*) was available as a late-season option; net bhp was rated at 190. Optional Conteur seats (*opposite, bottom*) helped forgetful types remember what they were driving.

potency of the engines, noting that "Brute power is out. Precision is in." In keeping with the fuel-conscious times, they also advised that "Excess is out. Efficiency is in."

With so much going for it, the third-generation Camaro was predictably little altered for 1983, its first full model year. The main mechanical change was addition of a new five-speed manual transmission as standard equipment for the V-6 Berlinetta and carbureted Z28, also available at extra cost for the four-cylinder base model. Shift linkages for both the four- and five-speed manuals got a new single-rail mechanism for reduced effort and smoother action. Later in the year, a four-speed overdrive automatic transmission joined the drivetrain availability chart. Geared for economy, this unit featured a torque converter clutch that locked up in all ratios except first to minimize gas-eating converter slip, an idea also applied to the '82 Corvette. Chevrolet made a high-output L69 305-cid V-8 with four-barrel

carburetor available as a late-season option, boasting more horsepower than even the "fuelie" engine. A total of 3223 H.O. engines were installed this year, out of a total production of 62,100 Z28s and 154,381 Camaros. Installation of CFI V-8s dropped to 19,847, while 9550 Camaros were ordered with all-disc brakes (RPO J65).

Enthusiasts yearning for a manual-shift fuel-injected Z28 would have to wait a little longer. Chevy had problems with certifying this combination for 1982 and decided not to offer it for '83, fearing its expected ratings in government mileage tests would force the company to pay the dreaded "gas guzzler" tax on every car sold with the feature.

A Conteur passenger seat to match the driver's became a new option. When installed in Z28s, these were trimmed in a bold tri-color fabric with a repeating "Camaro" logo, in a style reminiscent of certain Recaro seats. Also new this year

was an optional cargo area cover, and optional mats were carpeted instead of plain rubber. Stereo radios offered electronic tuning.

The latest Camaro was now more of a road car in the European mold than the all-out straight-line screamer of prior years. In fact, Chevrolet offered a special export version, the Z28E, sold in France and Germany. Equipped with a less restricted 305 V-8 breathing through a specific four-barrel carburetor, it rode a tuned suspension that split the difference between the very firm settings on the domestic Z28 and the softer Berlinetta chassis. The advent of the Z28E marked a first for Camaro: its emergence as a true GT at home anywhere in the world.

Despite its international flavor, Camaro remained very definitely American and a unique entity in the Chevrolet line. More importantly, it continued to express the ideas that had won its predecessors such wide acceptance in the Sixties and Seventies. In Chevrolet's words, the restyled Camaro "captures the essence of the contemporary American performance expression." At the same time, a 1980 survey had revealed that close to 37 percent of Camaros were purchased by women—far above the industry average. It was information like this that moved Chevy to the realization that Camaro had to be a multi-purpose machine with a selection of personalities.

Already, some convertible fans were eyeing the new coupe and imagining its top snipped off, now that Buick and Chrysler had reintroduced the ragtop. A handful of companies took the logical next step, and began to offer convertible conversions—tempting but expensive. Racing had gained prominence in advertising, and a number of special engine and suspension components were available for SCCA and other competition events.

So, was this upstart Camaro still a ponycar? Anyone in doubt had only to slip down behind the wheel, gaze out over the long hood, adjust the comfy bucket seat, twist the key, throw the shifter into first, and head for the nearest winding two-lane road. After a test drive, that "doubting Thomas" almost certainly would agree that the Camaro was not only a ponycar in the classic sense, but quite possibly the best Camaro ever built. Undeniably, early third-generation models suffered from indifferent assembly quality and, like many first-year editions, proved less than perfect. As we shall see, however, Chevy's ponycar kept getting better as the decade wore on.

Chapter Seven

Berlinetta Goes Digital: Futuristic Excess in '84

Since the beginning, Chevrolet had sought to market its 2+2 coupe to more than one type of customer. All-out performance buffs had their Z28s, of course; but when the year-end totals came in, non-Z Camaros took the lion's share of sales. Furthermore, V-6 engines were capturing more than one-third of that total. The influence of female buyers could hardly be ignored, either—not with well over one-third of Camaros being purchased by women.

As the mid-1980s approached, too, computers were capturing the attention of Americans. Not just the computers that sat upon office desktops, but the tiny ones that controlled engine and transmission functions in every modern automobile. Cars were also gaining more convenience gadgetry, much of it electronically controlled. Sci-fi films were filled with control panels and video screens. No surprise, then, that Chevrolet chose to capitalize on this evident phenomenon and create a digital dashboard for its mid-range Camaro, the Berlinetta.

Lagging well behind its two mates in sales, the Berlinetta was ripe for a fresh image. When the '84 arrived sporting its futurethink, sci-fi cockpit, observers were awed. Or in many cases, horrified. What Chevrolet unabashedly described as "space-age instrumentation" ranged from digital readouts to twin adjustable fingertip-operated control panels and a pivoting pedestal-mount radio. The Corvette-inspired cockpit also sported a roof console and adjustable low-back seats. "Camaro's continuing assault on the senses adds another dimension," Chevrolet proclaimed, presumably with pride, of the "High-Tech Berlinetta."

A digital display ahead of the driver showed road speed (in miles or kilometers per hour, with a top readout of 85 mph) plus either an odometer reading, trip odometer mileage, or precise engine speed. An adjoining vertical-bar tachometer gave the approximate rpm, flashing more urgently as engine speed climbed into "yellow line" range—and faster still at "red line" level. Another monitor with stacked warning lights, farther to the right, signaled low fluid levels or other possible trouble spots. Seven "telltales" lit in sequence as the engine started, followed by an "OK" light that lit briefly. Then, during driving, the lights functioned as ordinary indicators. Oddly, this electronic layout blended with a set of ordinary mechanical needle-type gauges at the left, which measured oil pressure, fuel level, coolant temperature, and voltage.

Each of the twin control pods could be moved closer to the steering wheel—just a fingertip away, if desired. The left pod contained switches for lights and instrument displays; the other held buttons for windshield wiper operation (above) and climate control (below), including a lever-type temperature selector. Setting the time-delay wipers was a trifle different than before, too. Tap the button once and the delay was set for 20 seconds. Tap it again a little later, and the interval would be set for the time *between* those two taps. Touch it once more and the memory would cancel. Chevrolet insisted that these pods amounted to "dual sliding computer terminals," part of the car's "aircraft-type precision ergonomics."

Additional pushbuttons resided in the floor console, to operate various optional features (if installed), including a remote rear-hatch release, rear defogger, rear wiper/washer, and power windows. Up above, the overhead console contained a swivel map light, dome light, penlight, and a small net storage pouch for cigarettes, sunglasses, or a garage door opener. Drum-type "reminder" spools also rode up there, with heading categories that were supposed to let you recall appointments, things to do, and so forth—just in case you got so wrapped up in the operation of the instrument panel that you forgot where you were headed.

Operating buttons for Berlinetta's optional cruise control sat on the steering wheel, but the system's on/off switch lurked down on the console. Other Chevrolets got a new form of stalk-mounted cruise control this year, which increased speed by one mph when you tapped one switch, or dropped by one mph with each tap of the end switch.

Either the driver or the passenger could grab the pedestal-mounted radio and swivel it over to his or her side. The mount was built into the floor console, while the receiver itself hid beneath that console. An electronically tuned AM/FM stereo radio with digital clock was standard on Berlinettas. Extra dollars bought a tape player and graphic equalizer for the pleasure of audiophiles.

All this gadgetry could be entertaining, and even informative—as Chevrolet promised—but it didn't necessarily improve one's kinship with the car. While intriguing, the buttons were simply too numerous and inadequately identified, and the digital readouts not easy to decipher at a glance.

"Bells, whistles, control pods everywhere!" declared Car and Driver magazine in its appraisal of the Berlinetta. "Zillions of little controlettes," all dressed in matte black with little to tell them apart. "With a full-zany, 21st-century treatment, the inside is now as spacey as the outside." Not only were sizes of the buttons too similar, but little color was used to differentiate the controls. In addition to that, C/D complained, the steering wheel tended to hide most of the twin-pod controls, which "hover on each side of the grippy steering wheel like .50-caliber-machine-gun handles." All told, the magazine's editors wondered why GM went this route, since it had been "obvious from the beginning that Chevrolet could sell its new generation of Camaros on looks alone." Answering their own question: "glitzy options" equal profits. Simple as that.

Road & Track advised readers that they'd really have to study this car before driving off—which of course isn't bad advice for *any* vehicle. Berlinetta aside, the magazine named the '84 Camaro one of the dozen top enthusiast cars, tied with Pontiac's Trans Am for best Sports GT in its price league.

High-tech gadgetry seemed to be
everywhere in the Eighties, and no one
was more preoccupied with it than
the designers of Camaro's Berlinetta.

Gadgetry apart, the '84 Berlinetta had a specific smooth-ride suspension, new tail-lamp moldings, and adjustable front head restraints. On the road, they were easy enough to spot with their gold-colored body trim. "Dollar for dollar," insisted Don Sherman of *Car and Driver*, "the Berlinetta stands up well against its toughest Japanese competition," with styling that amounted to "buy-me-now gorgeous."

Other changes for '84 were technical in nature, and generally more pleasing. A four-speed overdrive automatic replaced the earlier three-speed across the board, and

manual-shift Camaros added a hydraulic clutch to ease the strain on one's left foot. GM-specified "fourth-generation" all-season steel-belted radials went on all models except the "thoroughbred" Z28.

Performance of the Cross-Fire V-8 engine had proved disappointing, so it left the Z28 drivetrain list, replaced by the carbureted L69 high-output engine that had been added during 1983. With 9.5:1 compression, a higher-lift and longer-duration camshaft, free-breathing intake/exhaust and dual-snorkel cold-air induction, the L69 engine whipped up 190

Discreet gold striping made the 1984 Berlinetta easy to spot on the street. Attractive styling had been a Camaro selling point since the beginning, and with Berlinetta Chevy saw a chance to make money with a wealth of options. Love it or hate it, no one denied that the luxury Camaro had personality.

This page and opposite: Although "softer" in its appeal than its stablemates, the '84 Berlinetta was no less intriguing. Inside (*this page, top*) were twin control pods and an endless array of pushbuttons, levers, and digital doodads. V-8 (*above*) was optional.

with the rear seat folded down. In reality, that "deep-well luggage area" didn't hold quite as much as one might hope, and the broad expanse below the massive glass hatch was most useful only if cargo happened to be rather flat in shape. As always, too, passenger space in the rear was a painful joke. Still, no one bought a Camaro to fill it full of luggage or to shoehorn ordinary-sized people into the rear. They bought one for fun.

Chevrolet promoted the "best-selling" Sport Coupe as the only Chevrolet that came with a choice of four, six, or eight cylinders, with "clean aesthetics that some people think make it the purest Camaro." With the right options (F41 sport suspension, 5.0 V-8, Quiet Sound Group), a Sport Coupe was claimed to "give you the feel of Z28 with a hushed acoustical environment like Berlinetta."

Prices in '84 started at $7995 for a four-cylinder Sport Coupe, reaching $10,620 for a Z28 and $11,270 for a V-8 Berlinetta. Camaro production rose sharply this year, to a total of 261,591 (versus only 154,381 in the '83 model year). Evidently, 33,400 customers liked the digital dash enough to buy a Berlinetta. A total of 127,292 base Sport Coupes came off the line, along with an impressive 100,416 Z28s (plus 483 that went overseas as Z28Es).

Performance was gaining ground elsewhere in the Chevrolet line, too. The bigger Monte Carlo coupe added a high-performance SS model this year, and even the front-drive Celebrity offered a Eurosport option.

Ordinary Camaro shoppers might not have paid much attention at the time, but the International Race of Champions returned to the racing circuit during 1984, after a three-year absence. The announcement came in September 1983 that the IROC debut was scheduled for April 28, 1984, at Talladega International Speedway, to be followed by races at Michigan International Speedway and Riverside International Raceway. In these events, an even dozen of the world's top drivers—from NASCAR Grand National, Indy, and other motorsports—took to the track in identically prepared, thus evenly matched Z28s. Extensive TV coverage of the races by CBS Sports gave Camaro plenty of publicity, and Chevrolet was waiting in the wings with a street-legal edition that would borrow the IROC name. Armed with the knowledge that nearly two-thirds of Camaro buyers were under the age of 35, Chevy planned another assault on the youth market with its traditional ponycar.

horsepower. Other engines remained the same as before, including the 150-bhp LG4, which was standard on the Z28 and optional elsewhere. All powertrain combinations were available in all states, and any engine could have either a five-speed manual or four-speed overdrive automatic.

Chevrolet claimed a 0-60 mph time of 7.2 seconds with the high-output Z28 engine and five-speed manual shift, and a blast through the quarter-mile in 15.2 seconds. A Z28, they insisted, was "not a car that you merely drive. It's a car you

put on and wear with such authority that it changes your life forever." *Car and Driver* sent its automatic-equipped V-8 Berlinetta to 60 mph in 9.3 seconds, registering a speed of 80 mph in the quarter-mile after 17 seconds. Fuel mileage warranted groans, with a 14-mpg figure that stood far below the EPA's 21-mpg city/highway estimate.

Most of Camaro's third-generation pluses and minuses continued as before—and wouldn't change much for the remainder of its life. Cargo space, for one, looked impressive enough in print: 31.2 cubic feet

Chapter Eight

From Track to Street: The IROC-Z Arrives

Race-bred performance wasn't exactly a new idea in the mid-1980s. For years, both domestic and European automakers had taken technological advances that appeared on racing cars, then adapted them for production models. Now it was Chevrolet's turn to inject some added punch into its already-capable Z28 Camaro.

Camaros had returned to the track under the auspices of the International Race of Champions during 1984. A dozen identically prepped Camaros competed in four events at the hands of top race drivers with a variety of experience—NASCAR, CART, World Endurance Championship—to see who deserved credit as best of the best. At the same time, TV viewers got to see a selection of Camaros in action—Camaros that didn't look much different from the ones on sale down at the local Chevy dealership.

Looking closer, they were *a lot* different, of course, with tubular frames and fiberglass bodies instead of the usual assembly-line steel construction. Chassis built by Banjo Matthews were finished at Penske racing, where Jay Signore's group installed the engine, suspension, and running gear. Mechanical features for the race series included adjustable ride height and weight distribution, huge Hurst/Airheart disc brakes, a quick-change rear end, and 350-cid engines built by Katech in Mount Clemens, Michigan. With a 750-cfm carb, racers blasted around the Daytona oval at 187+ mph. The "ordinary" Holley 390-cfm carburetor helped churn up 420 horsepower and 400 pounds-feet of torque.

"The IROC race car is packing some heavy thunder," advised *Hot Rod* magazine, "but it drives like a Cadillac." A "Cadillac" that could accelerate to 60 mph in 5 seconds, that is, and run the quarter-mile in 13.4 seconds at 106 mph.

Yes, the street edition that emerged for 1985 was different from race versions, but it nevertheless incorporated a boatload of technical surprises. The IROC-Z was actually an option for the Z-28: IROC Sport Equipment Package (RPO B4Z). The option blended aggressive styling with invaluable chassis and drivetrain improvements. "This is really the culmination of the Z28—what we would have liked it to be from the beginning," Camaro engineer Phil Leistra told *Car and Driver*. Chevy called it "the Camaro that thinks it's a Corvette," a selling phrase that wasn't too far off the mark.

As *Motor Trend* declared in its preview test, an IROC-Z was meant "for the true Gonzo Camaro freak." Their testers ranked it "a responsive, precise, hard-cornering weapon that will humble many Euro/Japanese cars sporting much fancier window stickers." Summing up, the IROC-Z was "as good a racing street car as we have driven, with the exception of the Corvette."

"More than a commemorative model," explained *Car and Driver*, the IROC-Z qualified as "a champ in its own right." Comparable praise came from *Road & Track*, which noted that the street version "is born to run—quickly. And to handle . . . almost as well as its big brother, the Corvette."

Hot Rod magazine implicitly extended its praise to the Chevy execs responsible for Camaro's year-by-year improvement, explaining that the IROC-Z "positively confirms the ability of domestic automakers to get it right, provided they have enough chances to do it over." This one, they predicted, "may ultimately reign as the best Camaro ever built," a vehicle that "represents a competitive edge that defines the dimension between race car and street car—and narrows the gap between them."

With its fat P245/50VR16 Goodyear Eagle GT performance tires on big 16 × 8-inch five-spoke aluminum wheels, an IROC-Z rode about 15 millimeters lower than its Z28 partner (which wore 15 × 7 wheels). Tires wore unidirectional "gator-back" tread, as on the Corvette. IROCs also had higher-effort power steering and their own handling suspension, consisting of tighter front struts, springs and jounce bumpers, plus special rear springs and stabilizer bar. Delco-Bilstein gas rear shocks delivered a better ride and better control on rough roads. A new tubular cross member, known as a "wonderbar," bolted right below the regular anti-roll bar to provide extra front frame rail reinforcement, which minimized front-end chassis flexing. To improve straight-line stability, the front suspension's caster angle was adjusted to four degrees instead of the usual three.

Even from a distance, it wasn't hard to pick out an IROC-Z, which wore twin foglights within its grille and a lower-than-normal front air dam. Ornamental black louvers adorned the hood, while body-colored rocker panels and lower bodies displayed unique all-around striping. (Rockers were a contrasting color on ordinary Z28s.) Deep "ground effects" skirting encircled the whole car. IROC-Z decals sat low on each door. Camaro historian Michael Lamm reported that IROC-Z owners who didn't want to "advertise" might order one of the 502 examples that came from the California plant *sans* decals.

A new race-bred Camaro deserved a fresh engine, and that's precisely what the IROC-Z could have. The $659 basic price of the B4Z package bought the familiar L69 High-Output V-8 with four-barrel carburetion, offered only with a five-speed manual transmission—plus all the chassis tweaks and styling touches, of course. By paying a mere $695 above *that* price, you got something new: an LB9 variant, with Bosch tuned-port fuel injection (TPI), ready to whip out 215 horsepower—25 more than the basic IROC-Z powerplant—and an extra 35 pounds-feet of boisterous torque. Only Turbo Hydra-matic was available with that engine, however, which tacked another $395 onto the sticker price. According to some sources at the time, the hottest engine simply outmatched the torque-handling capability of the Borg-Warner T-5 five-speed manual used in other Camaros—a complaint that would rise again with the debut of the 5.7-liter V-8, late in 1986. Enthusiasts hoped for a manual-shift TPI Camaro, and analysts predicted that one would be forthcoming,

Race-bred and boasting a new name
and a new available V-8—that was
the IROC-Z, the Camaro performance
car that thundered onto the
scene for 1985.

The International Race of Champions lent its
acronym to Camaro beginning in 1985. The
IROC-Z was a Z28 option package that added
race-derived improvements to chassis and drivetrain.
The buff books seemed to agree that the car was
second only to Corvette for power and thrills. For
1986 (*above*) the IROC-Z could be had with a
5.7-liter V-8.

but it wasn't destined to be.

In the TPI engine, individually tuned runners channeled incoming air to each cylinder. Eight computer-controlled injectors supplied a precise amount of fuel to maintain optimum air/fuel ratio under all conditions. As described by *Motor Trend*, "pressure pulses arrive at the intake valve just as it opens, thus increasing cylinder filling." The ideal length of those runners turned out to be 21.5 inches, allowing peak power to develop about 400 rpm slower than on the carbureted engine. Among other modifications, the higher-lift, longer-duration cam kept the valves open for 320 degrees instead of the customary 300. Anyone glancing under the hood couldn't help but notice, too, that the tuned-port setup displayed looks to match its stunning performance.

Operating with hot-wire mass airflow sensor technology, the LB9 V-8 was a close relative of the larger Corvette engine. In fact, according to *Car and Driver* the LB9

originally was planned for installation in Corvettes, but went to Camaro/Firebird instead when it was determined that GM's two-seater needed the engine's full 5.7 liters.

Only the IROC-Z could get the 190-bhp L69 engine, incidentally. Regular Z-cars were limited to the 155-bhp engine, or to the top-dog TPI V-8.

Chevrolet claimed a TPI IROC-Z could zoom to 60 mph in about seven seconds, and travel the quarter-mile in around 15 seconds. *Road & Track* came close to those figures with the 215-bhp engine, hitting 60 in 7.3 seconds but requiring 15.8 for the quarter-mile. *Hot Rod* did a little better with the TPI, squeezing out a 0-60 mph run in 6.87 seconds, with a quarter-mile time of 15.3 seconds at 89.1 mph. All told, *Hot Rod* ranked the IROC-Z "a street fighter with all the right moves. . . . handsome, powerful, and agile with a gentleman's finesse."

"The new motor, quite simply, is a gem," said *Car and Driver* of the TPI V-8.

"When you snap your throttle foot down, the exhaust barks and you get shoved in the back as if you were in a barroom brawl." Their tester managed the 0-60 dash in a flat seven seconds, and traversed the quarter-mile in 15.2 seconds (reaching 91 mph), very close to Chevy's claims. As for handling, the IROC's "fat tires seem to stick as if they had been dipped in glue." The car "keeps all four paws firmly planted, even over bombed-out pavement." Noting that "all traces of crudeness" were gone, *C/D*'s final verdict said it all: "Without a doubt, the IROC-Z is the best all-around Camaro ever."

Not that the "lesser" L69 engine was a slouch. With a five-speed gearbox, *Car and Driver* sent its test L69-equipped Camaro to 60 mph in 7.5 seconds, and through the quarter-mile in 15.4, hitting 90 mph in the process. At 13 mpg overall, however, fuel mileage wasn't much of an improvement.

Though overshadowed by the IROC-Z,

Opposite and above: The 1985 IROC-Z was distinguished by twin foglamps and a front air dam that rode lower than normal. Discreet buyers could request that the door-mounted IROC-Z decals be dispensed with. The aluminum wheels looked great, and reviewers raved about the road-hugging ability of the fat tires.

"ordinary" Camaros also enjoyed a few pleasant changes for 1985. A new multiport fuel-injected version of the 2.8-liter V-6 engine went into the Berlinetta, yielding 135 horsepower (versus only 107 bhp for the carbureted '84 version). Compression of the basic LG4 V-8 jumped from 8.6:1 to 9.5:1, and Electronic Spark Control was added, raising horsepower by five. Suspension refinements included rear torque arm modifications as well as tweaked bushings, spring rates, and shock valving. All V-8s now had aluminum radiators and every Camaro carried "wet-arm" wind-

shield wipers, with washer outlets mounted on the blades. Split rear seatbacks (RPO AM9) were a new option. Popular extra-cost add-ons again included a rear spoiler (D80) for the Sport Coupe and Berlinetta, and removable glass roof panels (CC1) for all models. Any of the three models might have Berlinetta's overhead roof console (DK6), including those curious "reminder spools" with categories for range and distance, as well as such topics as Recreation and Business.

The Sport Coupe wore a new grille and front fascia, with a lower-riding air dam. A four-speed manual gearbox no longer was available, so every manual transmission now had five forward ratios including overdrive. All Z28s got a new, more rounded nose, a deeper front air dam, and lower rocker skirts. Inside were new speedometer graphics.

Berlinetta stuck with its futuristic electronic dashboard, but sales slumped badly—and would sink lower yet in 1986,

the model's final season. Echoing the comparison of the IROC-Z with Corvette, Chevy promoted the Berlinetta as "the luxury Camaro that thinks it's a Caprice." Not enough customers agreed, evidently. For that matter, total Camaro production dropped by nearly a third for the 1985 model year.

Changes were less dramatic for 1986. Sport Coupe buyers no longer needed to feel inferior, however, since—in Chevrolet's words—the "lowest-priced Camaro develops a Z28 snarl." When ordered with anything other than the four-cylinder engine, the base coupe now came equipped with a sport suspension comparable to the Z28's, P215/65R15 raised-letter blackwall tires on 15 x 7 styled steel wheels, and a performance axle ratio. A sport-tone exhaust with twin tailpipes let passersby know they were in the presence of an apparent powerhouse. Five-speed manual came with the V-6 version; four-speed automatic with V-8 Sport Coupes. Even four-cylinder Camaros got the sport suspension this time around, but rode 14-inch wheels.

Sport Coupes adopted a tougher look as well, with their black sport mirrors, rockers and fascia, and lower body striping. Headlamps and front vents added black accents this year, as did the taillamps. Out back, "Chevrolet" lettering replaced the former "Camaro" nameplate. Camaro's full-opening rear hatch now closed itself automatically—a helpful addition since that hatch was heavy. Softer-feel leather was installed on the steering wheel, gearshift lever, and parking brake lever. Halogen foglamps (as on the IROC-Z) were now available on all models, and all but the Sport Coupe could get bodyside moldings in a choice of eight colors. Z28 tires were redesigned to reduce rolling resistance. Like all cars in '86, Camaros added a center high-mount stop-

light, to comply with federal regulations.

Fuel mileage had long been a sore point with Camaro owners—and the car's critics—so two new items joined the standard equipment list for 1986 to make the car a bit more frugal. An upshift indicator light now informed manual-shift drivers when to snap into the next gear to get the greatest fuel economy; and for times when full power was needed, an air conditioning cutout switch was activated if the accelerator were tromped while the air was running.

Appearances can deceive, especially when you peek under a performance car's hood. Although it looked nearly the same as the '85, the '86 IROC-Z suffered a loss in potency. The tuned-port induction engine lost 25 horsepower, slipping back to the same 190-bhp rating as the high-output carbureted V-8. That detuned status occurred because Chevy substituted the

The IROC-Z had its roots in the 1984 International Race of Champions, (below), in which a dozen identically prepped Camaros driven by top drivers went head-to-head in a series of four events. Television viewers saw the best drivers from NASCAR, CART, and other circuits. Along the way, of course, those same viewers also got an eyeful of all those great-looking, hot-performing Camaros. These were true race cars, to be sure, with engine, suspension, and chassis modifications that were much different from the cars' showroom counterparts. Still, the competing cars were Camaros, and much of what was learned in their development and competition use was applied to the IROC-Z (opposite); the one pictured here is an '86.

camshaft from the lower-rung LG4 cam V-8 for the Corvette cam that had been employed in 1985. Torque output, on the other hand, edged upward by 10 pounds-feet, so an IROC-Z still was capable of some mighty fine motion when stomping the gas pedal. Under regular Z28 hoods, the standard LG4 engine delivered 10 more horses than when it was installed in a Sport Coupe or Berlinetta.

Late in the '86 season, Chevrolet sprung another surprise on Camaro fans, announcing availability of the Corvette's 350-cid (5.7-liter) V-8. Introduction was delayed for a time, and only a few were installed by the time the model year ended.

Already, rumors were floating around that Chevrolet was planning a shorter front-wheel-drive replacement for the Camaro/Firebird, expected late in the 1980s. Some observers believed the flashy GTZ show car, which appeared at the Specialty Manufacturers Association Show in Las Vegas, might be the next Camaro Z28. In reality, the GTZ was a showcase for the 90-degree V-6 engine.

After a year's delay, Chevrolet also introduced for 1986 a small-scale rival to Camaro's Z28: the front-drive Cavalier Z24. Though attracting its own legion of fans, the Z24 was no Camaro. Following a trial with a pre-production '86 Camaro and an equivalent Mustang, *Hot Rod* magazine ranked Camaro as "still the best handling production sport coupe in America." And more fun was soon to come in the popular ponycar.

The IROC-Z continued to be a potent street performer for 1986 (*above and opposite*), though bhp of the tuned-port induction V-8 was now rated at 190, down ten from 1985. The begadgeted Berlinetta (*below*) had become downright elegant looking by this time, but sales were down sharply, and Berlinetta would not return for '87. Some observers wondered if Camaro's traditional rear-drive configuration would return; front-drive was predicted by some.

Camaro Engine Options 1985

Engine type	ohv I-4	ohv V-6	ohv V-8	ohv V-8	ohv V-8
Code	LQ9	LB8	LG4	L69-HO	LB9
Bore x stroke (in.)	4.00 x 3.00	3.50 x 2.99	3.74 x 3.48	3.74 x 3.48	3.74 x 3.48
Displacement (L/cu. in.)	2.5 /151	2.8/173	5.0/305	5.0/305	5.0/305
Compression	9.0:1	8.9:1	9.5:1	9.5:1	9.5:1
Fuel delivery	TBI	MFI	4 bbl.	4 bbl.	TPI
Net bhp @ rpm	88 @ 4400	135 @ 5100	155 @ 4200	190 @ 4800	215 @ 4400
Torque (lbs-ft) @ rpm	132 @ 2800	165 @ 3600	245 @ 2000	240 @ 3200	275 @ 3200

For 1986, the LG4 engine was rated 165 bhp and 250 lbs-ft when installed in a Z28. The LB9 V-8 dropped to 190 bhp @ 4000 rpm, but its torque rose to 285 lbs-ft @ 2800 rpm.

Chapter Nine

California Dreamin':
Camaro Goes Topless

Cynics who claimed that Camaros "never change" had some surprises in store during the final years of the Eighties. More surprises than in 1985, in fact, when the blast-off IROC-Z first topped the Camaro performance lineup, establishing a link with Chevrolet's two-seat Corvette. The eager, race-derived IROC-Z coupe was back in '87, soon obliterating its Z28

parent. Yet the IROC's success was just part of a memorable new chapter in the Camaro story—a chapter that began with a bigger V-8 and a convertible conversion.

Performance takes precedence for the typical Camaro fan, and Chevrolet had good news in that direction. Announced during the 1986 model year, the big (for the Eighties) 5.7-liter V-8, lifted from the

Corvette, was now available in full force under Camaro hoods. By the end of the 1987 model year, a whopping 12,105 of the mighty tuned-port L98 V-8s had been installed in IROC-Z Camaros—close to one-fourth of total Z28 production.

Eager to churn out 225 horsepower and a muscular 330 pounds-feet of torque, the 5.7-liter V-8 used a tuned-port fuel-

More power, continued refinement of already great looks, and the welcome return of the ragtop were Camaro highlights as the Eighties drew to a close.

injection system, like the smaller TPI engine. The basic Z28 had a 170-hp four-barrel carbureted 305-cid (5.0-liter) V-8 as standard fare, with a new five-speed manual gearbox for 1987. Sure, the 5.7 V-8 cost an extra $1045, but what was an extra thousand or so when all that oomph lay in wait beneath the gas pedal? As had been the case with the smaller TPI V-8,

though, the bigger mill was available only with four-speed overdrive automatic. No manual-shift edition was offered, either in '87 or later. That 5.0-liter TPI engine, incidentally, cost $745 extra; so it was only a modest financial step up to the big boy. On the other hand, after a one-year drop to 190 horsepower, the LB9 TPI V-8 returned to its initial 215-bhp rating.

The 1988 IROC-Z convertible (*below*) combined brute power with the allure of top-down motoring. These were conversions executed for Chevy by the California facility of Michigan-based ASC Inc. The convertibles weren't cheap, mainly because of the expense of necessary structural adjustments and bracing, but sales topped 5600 for '88. Of that number, more than two-thirds were IROC-Zs.

With manual shift, that is; automatic-transmission TPI models got the less-potent powerplant.

"Leaner and meaner" was Chevrolet's description for the most powerful edition. "America's favorite sport coupe . . . is a meaner hombre in '87 with the arrival of the 5.7 liter TPI V8 powerplant roaring under the hood of the hot IROC-Z." Earlier IROCs couldn't get air conditioning, but that option soon became available for "the ultimate Camaro."

Whether installed in the 5.0- or 5.7-liter engine, tuned-port injection was designed to give instant throttle response, dependable operation (thanks to few moving parts), reduced maintenance, and reliable "hot starts." The system's self-adjusting idle increased speed automatically with accessories on; positive fuel shut-off prevented "run-on."

With all these tempting engine choices at hand, the L69 high-output carbureted V-8 dropped out of the drivetrain selection. Four-cylinder power also became a relic of the short-lived past, as the Generation II edition of GM's 173-cid (2.8-liter) V-6 became the base Camaro powerplant. Sales of Camaros with the Pontiac "Iron Duke" four had started out strongly enough in 1982, when the third generation debuted, but shrunk steadily afterward. Base and LT Camaros could have a 165-bhp version of the four-barrel LG4 V-8 engine. Except

The venerable Z28 (*opposite, top*) and the IROC-Z (*this page, below*) returned for '87. A tuned-port injection V-8 (*above*) was now available on the IROC. Base models (*opposite, bottom*) ran with a 173-cid V-6.

An RS (Rally Sport) Camaro (*this page and opposite*) became available as a California-only option early in 1987. Only three colors were available: red, white, and black, with color-coordinated wheels. Although the RS shared body cladding and other visual cues with the Z28, it was a much milder car, running with the 2.8-liter V-6 as standard. But the *appearance* of power had always been important to a segment of the Camaro audience, and the RS turned out to be a sound bit of marketing.

for the IROC-Z with 5.7-liter V-8, all Camaros could have either a five-speed manual gearbox or four-speed overdrive automatic.

Nameplates got a two-edged shuffling this year as the Berlinetta finally dropped out, a victim of sagging sales, replaced by a set of option packages that created a new LT model. Actually, the LT designation had been used in the Seventies for Camaro's midrange model, until it was usurped by the Berlinetta in 1979. So turnabout was fair play once again. Marketed by ordering code RPO (Regular Production Option)

B4E, the LT option included the V-6 engine and a selection of comfort/convenience extras: Quiet Sound Group, Custom cloth interior, air conditioning, AM/FM stereo with seek/scan, tinted glass, Comfortilt steering wheel, and auxiliary lighting. LTs wore body-colored sport mirrors, upper and lower body striping, and full wheel covers within their all-season 14-inch tires. A "Boulevard-ride" suspension and quieter exhaust gave the LT a more civilized demeanor than its more raucous mates, befitting its role as the "grand touring" Camaro.

Supreme stereo could add as much as $1088 to the sticker price. Even on the IROC-Z, standard equipment included only an AM radio; anything in stereo cost extra. The addition of a leather option was accompanied by the loss of optional Lear Siegler Conteur seating.

Appearance revisions were minor for '87, limited mainly to striping modifications. Those who yearned to toughen the look of their Sport Coupes again had the option of such add-ons as a rear spoiler ($69), removable T-roof panels ($866), and slick rear-window louvers ($210). Spoiler-equipped Camaros now had their center stoplight mounted at that location, instead of on the hatch glass. An audible headlamp-on warning tone was now standard.

Sport Coupes were described as "Camaro at its most elemental," and plenty of customers wouldn't have it any other way, easily steering clear of Z28/IROC-Z temptations—and their higher price tags. With its tight suspension and throaty sport-tone exhaust, even a V-6 Sport Coupe had the look and sound of a thoroughbred. Only the initiated would know the difference anyway, especially with a couple of those extra-cost accessories strategically placed on the base coupe's epidermis.

"Chevy thunder" was a marketing theme for 1987, and to no one's surprise, the company focused on Camaro's performance potential. "Camaro is a driving energy," the copywriters exclaimed, "untamed and seeking challenge at every turn." The coupe's "svelte curves embody independence," with aero styling that "is at once sensual and aggressive, but then . . . aren't you?" Quite a few car-shoppers in 1987 evidently decided they were.

As before, the IROC-Z was actually an option package (RPO B4Z) for the Z28. For $669, it brought such goodies as P245/50VR16 Goodyear Eagle GT tires on 16-inch aluminum wheels, front frame reinforcement, specific steering gear valving, a unique front suspension, and modified rear suspension with larger-diameter stabilizer bar and gas-filled Delco/Bilstein shock absorbers. Once again, IROCs were identified by body-color "ground effects" panels, grille-mounted foglamps, door panel decals, and lower-body accent striping. Unidirectional rubber helped achieve (according to Chevrolet) an impressive .88g lateral acceleration on the skidpad. Not many owners really had to have that level of capability in their daily commutes, of course, but it was nice to know it was available—just in

California customers had yet another option choice starting early in 1987. An RS Camaro (picking up the Rally Sport designation from an earlier time) appeared at the Los Angeles Auto Show, and went on sale as a Special Equipment Order option package. Styling details were similar to the Z28, including rocker-panel extensions, lowered suspension, and body-colored chin spoiler. Under the RS hood, however, lay the same 2.8-liter V-6 used in the Sport Coupe. Only three colors were available: red, white, and black, with color-coordinated rocker panels and wheels.

Customers also were required to order several extra-cost options, including air conditioning and a rear spoiler.

California was the sole market for the RS because executives in Michigan wanted to see how it caught on before expanding availability nationwide. That wouldn't happen for a couple more years.

Luxury touches appeared elsewhere, too. A Delco-GM Bose sound system was now available, with acoustics tailored specifically for the Camaro interior. Leather seating became available for the first time in a Camaro. Neither option came cheap.

case you got trapped in a high-speed turn on the way to the office.

Road & Track magazine had a lot of praise for the IROC-Z with the L98 engine option, praise that went beyond the car's sterling performance. "The Chevy V-8," they said, "is tuned to produce that particularly American burble emitted by every V-8 that was ever given a set of dual pipes and glass packs." In addition to "styling that remains a work of art," with "one of the most sensuously curved hoods in existence," the top Camaro delivered "unflappable handling" and "soul-stirring throb." Add to these attributes a 0-60 acceleration time of 6.8 seconds, and 15.3 seconds for the quarter-mile, and it's safe to say that road-testers were more than pleased. Chevrolet's own estimate was a bit more optimistic: 0-60 in about 6.3 seconds, and the quarter-mile run in as little as 14.5.

Not long after the debut of the third-generation Camaro for 1982, custom shops had begun to contemplate snipping off the top to create a Camaro convertible. Some of them actually did so. Now it was time for an "official" ragtop to rejoin the ranks, after an 18-year absence. "The Camaro body shape," declared *Road & Track*, "is a natural for a ragtop." And so it was.

When convertibles re-entered the market in the early 1980s, led by Chrysler, most were crafted not by the automakers themselves but by independent outside organizations. One of the most capable was Automobile Specialty Company (a division of ASC Inc.), which had first gained renown for its aftermarket sunroofs. ASC started on the Camaro project as another aftermarket idea, before gaining official sanction from Chevrolet. That approval allowed ASC to plan on building a substantially larger number of ragtops at its facility in City of Industry, California.

Conversion of a T-roofed coupe into a convertible wasn't a simple matter of slicing off the steel top and tacking on some canvas, of course. Even though the T-top was already stiffer than a standard coupe, a considerable quantity of strengthening material had to be incorporated into the

By the late Eighties, second-generation Camaro styling was showing its age. Still, topless versions like the base-model '88 (*opposite, top*) were aggressively beautiful. The '87 IROC-Z (*opposite, bottom*) lived up to that year's "Chevy thunder" ad campaign: With the optional 350-cid L98 engine, the IROC could zip from 0-60 in less than 7 seconds. Exceptional handling was just icing on the cake.

car's structure, to minimize the likelihood of flex as the car rolled over uneven pavement. Camaro expert Michael Lamm notes in his detailed history, *Camaro—The Third Generation*, that "structural gussets and braces had to be added to the inner floorpan, the inner rear quarters, and the outer rockers [plus] inner floorpan/rocker reinforcements that tied into both the A- and B-pillars." Only then could attention be paid to the manual folding top itself, hidden beneath a rear-hinged deck and originally designed with Corvette in mind. Instead of the customary glass hatch, convertible buyers actually got a usable trunk, with no loss of space in the rear seat, either—style and practicality, all in one shot. Offered in base, Z28, and IROC-Z trim, a soft top added some $4400 to the car's cost. Base prices started at $9995 for a V-6 Sport Coupe and stretched to $12,819 for a Z28 coupe and $13,488 for the IROC-Z option. Even so, just over a thousand Camaro fans checked RPO Z08 to get a convertible in 1987.

Convertibles caught hold with a vengeance the next year, when 5620 were produced (two-thirds of them in IROC-Z dress). Both convertibles shared a three-piece rear spoiler with stoplamp, which extended forward onto the rear surface of the doors. "Out on the street," said *Motor Trend* of the late-Eighties ragtop, "no one doesn't notice this car."

Glancing at the '88 showroom selection must have produced a few bewildered countenances among Camaro fans, as there was nary a Z28 to be found. Only the base Sport Coupe and IROC-Z made the lineup this time, the latter officially listed as a model unto its own, usurping the famed Z28 designation. Well, actually it remained part of the ordering code for an IROC-Z, but that was hardly the same thing. Also missing this year was the LT option package, which hadn't lasted long at all as Berlinetta's replacement.

As the "real" Z28 departed, the base coupe added several intriguing items of standard equipment to give it a Z28 demeanor, including a rear spoiler, accent-colored lower body panels, aluminum wheels, and body-color mirrors (formerly black). At the Sport Coupe's rear was a Z28-style fascia that held a new one-piece spoiler with stoplight. An AM/FM stereo radio with seek/scan was now standard, and the new full-gauge instrument cluster included a 115-mph speedometer. Inner door panels were now formed of one-sided galvanized steel, for greater corrosion resistance. Vinyl seat trim was gone,

replaced by cloth even at base level.

Base Sport Coupe power came again from the 2.8-liter V-6, now rated at 125 horsepower. The optional 305-cid (5.0-liter) V-8 lost its carburetor, turning instead to throttle-body fuel injection. That brought a net gain of five horsepower.

The standard IROC-Z engine was the LO3 V-8, ready to deliver 170 horsepower. IROC-Z customers had two additional tuned-port-injection choices, however: a high-output version of the 5.0-liter V-8, rated at 220 horsepower with five-speed manual shift (but only 195 horsepower with automatic), or the Corvette-based 350-cid (5.7-liter) edition, which again came only with a four-speed overdrive automatic transmission.

IROC-Z Camaros had their own lower-bodyside accent striping, wheels, tires, interior trim, and new options. Decals moved to the rear of each door. Standard 15-inch aluminum wheels held black-letter Eagle GT tires, with 16-inchers optional. Like the Sport Coupe, the IROC-Z had a 115-mph speedometer with the standard V-8 engine.

Conservative-minded IROC-Z customers could avoid the attention-drawing stripes and decals by grabbing the order sheet and checking DX3, an RPO code that deleted the offending identifiers.

"Not only has the car aged gracefully," said *Road & Track* of the '88 Camaro, "but it also has made the transition to convertible smoothly." With a 215-bhp V-8 and five-speed, *RT* testers managed a 0-60 mph trek in 6.6 seconds. Quarter-mile time came to 14.9 seconds, with a 95-mph final speed. Quick it was, though "definitely not the quietest car we've tested." For Camaro lovers, that wasn't necessarily a criticism. Those harsh sounds might be jarring to some, but a welcome melody to others, who'd feel uncomfortable in a Camaro that was eerily silent.

Musclecar Review magazine advised that the basic V-8 Sport Coupe was "responsive, handles well and brakes competently. Inside, the ergonomics are excellent." On the whole, this was "a tight, well thought-out package with few faults. . . . until you open the hood."

"Around town," *MCR* continued, "the low-end torque characteristics of the LO3, combined with the T-5 five-speed's ratios and 3.42:1 rear gears make the Camaro Sport Coupe feel like a real hunk from stoplight to stoplight. The throbbing exhaust and the neck-snapping off-the-line acceleration give the impression there's more than 170 horses there." Yet "on the

track, the Camaro falls flat on its flexible nose." Then again, how many Sport Coupe owners spent time hauling the car around a race track?

Braking had long been a sore point among Camaro critics. Not everyone was satisfied with the optional four-wheel disc system on a car that was otherwise so capable. Another problem that bothered Camaro owners who raced their machines was a propensity for the engine to "starve" on tight curves. To deal with both complaints, Chevrolet introduced a special option late in the 1988 model year, little known to the typical Camaro fancier but vital to the competition-minded. Known by its RPO code number (1LE), the option package included Corvette-style, twin-piston aluminum calipers made by Australia's PBR Automotive; the calipers had 12-inch rotors, versus the usual 10.5-inch units. With fewer moving parts, the new brake setup was created to deliver quicker pad release with less drag, and more even pad wear. Also included was a revised gas tank and pickup, intended for

reliable operation during high-g cornering. Offered as a limited-production item, 1LE was available only in conjunction with certain other options.

So where did Camaro rate in its perennial battle with rival Mustang? Through much of 1988, Ford earned a 2-to-1 sales lead, according to *Musclecar Review*. Final total: just six Camaros sold for every 10 Mustangs. Camaros also were subject to "astronomical surcharges" on insurance, because of their attractiveness to thieves, the youthfulness of many buyers, and the likelihood of some owners to hit the gas pedal a little too hard and too often. These insurance costs help explain the reason for the debut of the RS series with its standard V-6 power.

Introduced during 1987 as a California choice, the RS designation took over the base coupe's spot in the Camaro lineup for 1989. The RS (Rally Sport) nameplate actually dated back to an option on the first (1967) Camaros. This one mixed some IROC-Z styling touches with the more modest power of a V-6 or low-end V-8

engine. RS Camaros included body-colored lower aero panels, dual sport mirrors, new P215/65R15 "touring" tires on Z28-style cast aluminum wheels, and a specific rear spoiler. Performance equipment included a sport suspension with front/rear stabilizer bars, quick-ratio power steering, and a standard 5-speed manual gearbox. Automatic transmission was optional. Sales literature called RS the "dressy coupe that combines artistry with sensibility."

To help combat thieves, Chevrolet introduced a "PASS-key" (Personal Automotive Security System) theft-deterrent system as standard equipment. Introduced on the '86 Corvette, that system had brought about a noticeable drop in thefts, and would eventually prove similarly capable when installed in Camaros (and Firebirds). Unless the correct electronically coded key was inserted into the ignition, the engine would fail to start. A built-in time lag forced a 2-3 minute delay between attempts to start the car with the wrong key. Before long, some insurance companies began to offer discounts on a portion of coverage—

For 1988, the base Sport Coupe (*opposite*) was powered by the 2.8-liter V-6 rated at a modest 125 horsepower. The 305-cid V-8, now sans carburetor, was optional, and the Coupe picked up styling touches that were reminiscent of the Z28. A good thing, too, because the '88 IROC-Z (*above*) had usurped the Z28 altogether, and was now Camaro's only overtly muscular offering.

welcome news to Camaro owners who'd been paying massive premiums.

Both the open and closed IROC-Z, and the RS convertible, came with a standard 170-horsepower V-8. RS coupes stuck with the base V-6 engine and its adequate if uninspiring 135 horsepower. Once again, IROC-Z folks had two tempting powertrain choices to check on the options list: the 220-horsepower, 305-cid (5.0-liter) V-8, or the larger 350-cid (5.7-liter) V-8 with 10 extra horses. Both engines kept their tuned-port fuel injection systems, but the big one changed its ordering code from L98 to B2L.

At the IROC end of the spectrum, a new reduced back-pressure dual converter exhaust system became available for each

TPI V-8, adding 10 horsepower, while progressive throttle application was supposed to make the engine easier to control. Both engines got "Multec" fuel injectors for improved fuel atomization. In top tune, then, the 5.7-liter IROC-Z engine could deliver 240 bhp at 4400 rpm, and an energetic 345 pounds-feet of torque. Rear brakes on the optional all-disc system got larger rotors and Corvette-style aluminum calipers. IROCs also gained restyled standard 15-inch aluminum wheels and new optional Goodyear 16-inch unidirectional tires with Z speed rating, good for 150 mph or more.

"After a long, agonizing childhood," noted *Hot Rod* magazine of the 1989 IROC-Z, "the third-generation Camaro has nearly reached its full potential" and is "still one of the most beautiful cars made in America." The top-rung Camaro offered "swift, surefooted aggressiveness through the mountains, and it is still docile enough for your grandma to drive to her doctor's appointment." In a trial run with a 240-bhp version of the 5.7-liter engine, the

magazine's testers blasted to 60 mph in a startling 5.9 seconds.

Road & Track agreed that the "sexy, take-on-all-comers good looks" of Jerry Palmer's initial design had "admirably withstood the test of time. We all should hope to age so gracefully."

Analysts were always looking ahead to the next-generation Camaro. Some believed they spotted it in the lines of the California Camaro that appeared in 1989. Most were not lured into foolish statements, but accepted the show car for what it was: a pretty but far-from-practical styling exercise, intended mainly to show off the twin-cam V-6 engine. Created at the GM Advanced Design Concept Center at Santa Barbara, California, under the direction of John Schinella, the show car wore a metal body yet took only six months to build—from scale model to running automobile. "This may not be the real '92 Camaro," admitted *Hot Rod*, "but at least it confirms that they're on the right track in styling."

Chevy wasn't quite ready with its facelifted Camaro as the 1990 model year

Camaro has always inspired speculation about its future. In 1989, soothsayers had something tangible to jaw about: the "California Camaro" GTZ concept car. Although recognizably a Camaro, this metal-bodied, operational beauty suggested a new direction for Chevy's ponycar.

began, so changes were modest for this shortened season. A larger (3.1-liter) V-6 engine went into the RS coupe, replacing the long-lived 2.8-liter six. The new V-6 developed 144 horsepower at 4400 rpm, yielding 180 pounds-feet of torque. Not an enormous jump, but enough to make a difference when passing or merging.

A new speed-density control system on all engines gathered information from several sensors, calculating the amount of air and fuel needed to maintain proper ratio during warm-engine conditions. The 5.7-liter V-8 got reduced-weight pistons to boost efficiency and increase bearing durability. By this time, that biggest V-8 (RPO B2L) added only $300 to the price of an IROC-Z Camaro—less than the cost

of an optional V-8 for the RS coupe. An extra $466 bought a performance axle ratio with dual exhausts, plus all-disc brakes and an engine oil cooler.

All Camaros added a driver's airbag with knee bolsters. Camaros with four-speed overdrive automatic earned a tightened torque converter that operated with higher lockup points, to boost gas mileage —still not exactly a "plus" in the Camaro's list of attributes. Standard equipment now included halogen headlamps, tinted glass, intermittent wipers, and a Comfortilt steering wheel, plus 16-inch spoked alloy wheels on the IROC-Z convertible (optional on the coupe). Every IROC-Z also came with a limited-slip differential. Instrument panels displayed new yellow graphics.

No need to worry about stains inside, one would expect, with the new Scotchgard™ fabric protection. And ears that were unaccustomed to loud sounds might take a beating in a Camaro that happened to have the optional Delco/Bose II sound system with a digital disc player. Now

rated at 185 watts (almost twice the previous setup), the system's CD player had a "dynamic compression" feature to boost quiet passages and subdue loud ones. On the practical side, a new Delco "LOC" system disabled the disc player when disconnected from the battery, so it wouldn't play until a code was entered—a fine companion to the PASS-Key theft-deterrent. No point letting thieves enjoy the stereo, either.

So, how did the last examples of this interim period fare against their forerunners? Driving an IROC-Z, in the opinion of *Motor Trend*, was "like stepping back into the muscle-car era." The all-out Camaro "has the unmistakable rumble so dear to many hearts and provides the unequivocal delight from lots of cubic inches twisting that rear axle." Yet "this is a sophisticated muscle-car, made so by the miracle of the computer chip." And in contrast to earlier complaints about automatic-transmission operation, the 700R4 four-speed "happens to be one of the best automatics we've ever experienced," a unit

The RS took the place of the Sport Coupe in the 1989 lineup (*top*), and gained a new standard engine for 1990 (*middle*), a 3.1-liter V-6 rated at 144 horsepower. 1990 IROC-Zs (*above*) were protected by the PASS-key system that had been introduced for '89.

that "downshifts precisely when the driver would do so for himself in a manual gearbox." *MT* applauded the car's off-the-line prowess, described as "blazingly fast out of the hole," reaching 30 mph in a mere 2.2 seconds and 60 mph in just 5.8 seconds.

On the down side, *Motor Trend* continued, "high unsprung weight of the solid rear axle assembly is unquestionably difficult to control." That sort of lament was heard more and more, especially as Camaro was compared with the best of the front-drive performance-oriented machines that had appeared during the Eighties. "When the bumps get the axle moving, it bounds around back there with furious abandon, transmitting considerable amounts of noise and shock into the passenger compartment." At three-fourths of its potential, on the other hand, "the Camaro corners like the 20th Century Limited [once the most famous train in America]."

Road & Track cited the mere presence of the IROC-Z convertible as proof that at Chevrolet "true romantics still exist." Not that everything was A-1 in the soft-top arena. *R/T* wasn't at all pleased with the convertible top's imperfect sealing and poor fit at the rear deck; or by the lack of "structural integrity" that allowed testers to actually watch the cowl and dashboard move, and feel the shake in the steering wheel.

Opinion was far more positive when *Road & Track* took a turn in an IROC-Z coupe with the 1LE braking option. Stopping distance was no better than usual, but improved heat-absorption and thicker brake pads brought virtually no fade after extra-heavy operation. That option, on the other hand, wasn't really aimed at street driving.

Early in the 1990 model year, rumors were heard that Chevrolet no longer would be authorized to use the IROC name on its cars, and that the next IROC racing automobile would be a Dodge Daytona. *Motor Trend* speculated that the change could be due to the efforts of Jim Perkins, Chevrolet's new general manager, who preferred to promote corporate racing activities that involved competition with other makes, not rivalry within a single car model. In addition, IROC-Z sales had been falling, so its era as a valuable marketing tool appeared to have drawn to a close. As we shall see in the next chapter, the IROC connection indeed was in its final stage; but another famous nameplate was ready for a comeback.

Chapter Ten

Z Returns, With a Facelift: Trimming Down the Line

As Chevrolet's association with the International Race of Champions ceased at the end of 1989, a mildly facelifted Camaro was almost ready for the marketplace. Introduced in the spring of 1990 as an early '91 model, the final rendition of Jerry Palmer's third-generation design wasn't nearly as fresh as some had expected. While Pontiac stuck a new nose onto its Firebird, inspired by the Banshee show car, Chevrolet restricted Camaro to minor touch-ups: new front and rear fascia, new aero rocker moldings, a stoplight mounted under the rear hatch glass—and not a whole lot more.

What to call the high-performance edition, now that the IROC nameplate was out of bounds? What else but Z28? The decision revived the legendary name that had adorned race-bred Camaros as far back as 1967, but that was abandoned after 1987 when an "IROC" badge was thought to command more attention. Several special touches marked the resurrected Z-car, which wore its own style of aero-formed rear wing spoiler (except on the convertible), scooped lower locker panels, a red bow-tie emblem in its grille, and non-functional hood bulges. Lower-body striping and decals were consigned to the dustbin.

Beneath those hood bulges sat either the familiar 5.0-liter V-8 or the Corvette-derived 5.7-liter powerplant. The smaller engine was rated at 170 horsepower with ordinary fuel injection (code LO3), or 230 bhp with the tuned-port setup (LB9) and performance axle (205 bhp without). That performance ratio cost as much as $675 extra, in a package that included a dual exhaust system, bigger brakes, aluminum driveshaft, special shocks, and more. Formerly limited mainly to race fans, that option was now available to anyone willing to pay the extra dollars.

For extra get-up-and-go, the 5.7 V-8 (code B2L) stood ready to deliver 245 horses on command. Alloy 16-inch wheels on the Z28 displayed a fresh pattern, and were also available on the RS Camaro. The Z28 suspension enjoyed a tune-up.

Convertibles came in both levels: RS and Z28.

"Z28 is clean, mean," insisted Chevy's promotional writers. "No stripes. No decals. No nonsense. Just brilliant basecoat/clear-coat on one of the sleekest shapes in automotive history." When describing the "maximum Camaro," the ad writers tossed around such terms as "aggressive" and "outrageous" with abandon. Well, the expense of purchasing a new Camaro was certainly nothing to take lightly: A Camaro price tag slipped past the $20,000 mark in 1991, reaching $20,815 for the Z28 convertible. Throw in a handful of options, and you were talking real money.

Once again, the base RS coupe came equipped with a standard 3.1-liter V-6, but had the option of the least-potent V-8—the 5.0-liter. The standard stereo radio with cassette player added a "Search" feature and soft-touch controls. Otherwise, the changes consisted of details. Fluidic windshield wipers became standard; acoustics were improved, to cut road noise, and a quieter starter motor was installed.

Traditional-style analog instruments consisted of a large semicircular speedometer and 7000-rpm tachometer, with four small semicircular gauges filling the space between. Manual-shift fanciers again had a big, round gearshift knob at the ready. The RS Convertible came with standard V-8 power and a specially tuned suspension. The convertible's manually operated top slipped neatly beneath a fiberglass tonneau cover.

By the fall of 1990, base prices shot up $1185 on the RS coupe and $1080 on the convertible from their levels at the time of the spring debut, just months earlier. That doubtless didn't help sales much, or Camaro's perennial sales battle with Ford's Mustang—a battle that GM had been losing for some time. Sure, Camaros kept their value better than most, because young drivers tended to snap up the secondhand examples. Still, used-car sales don't add anything to the year-end reports that are perused in Chevy's executive offices.

By this time, too, the bloom seemed to have fallen off Camaro's rose, at least in the eyes of some experts. What might have been deemed lovable eccentricities a few years earlier appeared to have turned into annoyances. CONSUMER GUIDE® magazine was not alone in faulting the early-Nineties Camaro for its insistent exhaust note, poor gas mileage, punishingly stiff ride, and poor wet-road traction. For the everyday car buyer rather than the strict enthusiast, Camaros warranted little more than a lukewarm recommendation. Lack of anti-lock braking was a sore point, too, as ABS became available on a number of other GM models. Chevrolet sales literature promised that the "rear-wheel-drive design provides delightful balance and feel," but some former Camaro devotees were looking closer at modern front-drives.

Never a lightweight, Camaro gained even more poundage in this latest incarnation. Everyone knew, too, that while the design had improved through the life of the third generation, it still wasn't devoid of squeaks and rattles, and offered little space for cargo or back-seat passengers. Perhaps some of the folks who'd once expressed such fondness for the car were simply growing older.

Motor Trend ranked the latest Z28 (and Firebird Formula) among the top 10 performance cars when price was considered as a factor, but described the pair as not "as sophisticated as some others" on the list. With 0-60 times of 6.5 seconds or so, the pair were "still winners in our book." And with skidpad competence in the 0.87-0.89 range, handling was rated "truly stellar." Even an RS Camaro with the 170-bhp LO3 engine was able to reach 60 mph in 7.9 seconds, and "Camaro tackles the turns with a vengeance." All in all, *MT* determined, "few car designs have aged as well."

Car and Driver took a rather negative tone in its appraisal of the '91 Z-car, though performance ranked high. "Cruising around town," they noted, "the small-block [5.0-liter] V-8 grumbles just enough to gain

Although the Z28 nameplate returned
for 1991, Camaro was feeling its age,
as well as pressure levied by newer,
more sophisticated competitors.
Yet Camaro still had the power to thrill.

attention." Acceleration to 60 mph took a swift 6.4 seconds, 100 mph was hit in 17.6, whereas a dash through the quarter-mile was completed in 14.9 seconds. On the other hand, *C/D* testers complained of road and drivetrain noise, advised that "the body creaks and complains even during normal straight-line cruising." This "game but aging powerhouse," they summarized, comes rather close to being "crude."

Perhaps more to the point in an era when heavy rear-drive cars were viewed by some as antiquated engineering, how did a Camaro rate against front-drive rivals? In a comparison test of a Z28 with performance axle package against such hot cars as the Eagle Talon and Dodge Stealth R/T, *Motor Trend* offered the opinion that the "5-liter engine provides instantaneous and predictable response to throttle movement." Beyond that, the Z28 was "stable, fast, and possessed of an impressive amount of grip in the corners," while

The third-generation Camaro body, more than a decade old by the time of the '91 RS (*above*), retained its sleek, forceful appeal. A 3.1-liter V-6 was standard with the base RS, but Camaro's mildest V-8, the 5.0-liter, was an available option. The six cranked out a modest 140 horses, but acceleration from stoplights was certainly adequate, and "helped" by a tuned exhaust note.

"steering is particularly sharp and responsive, and the car is amenable to a variety of driving styles."

Of course, for those who wanted acceleration that felt like a blast into outer space, one or two specialty shops were stuffing an occasional 454-cid V-8 into that tempting space beneath a Camaro hood. "When you put your foot into the gas of an automatic 454 Camaro," *Motor Trend* exclaimed of its one-off machine, "that brawler takes off like an F/A-18 catapulted from the flight deck of the *Nimitz.*"

Camaros may have left the IROC scene, but did not abandon competition altogether. In May 1991, Camaro achieved its 50th SCCA Trans-Am race victory—more than any model in the 26-year history of that series.

. With the exception of a "Heritage Appearance" option package, available for $175 on all models to mark Camaro's 25th anniversary, little was new for the '92 model. Offered on both the coupe and convertible, the Anniversary edition came in Arctic White, Bright Red, or Black, and included bold hood and trunk-lid stripes, a body-colored grille and wheels, and black headlamp pockets. Instrument panels on all '92s—Heritage or not—contained a 25th anniversary emblem.

Convertibles were due for some improvements, including new rear lap/shoulder belts, an easier-opening top, rear courtesy lamps, and more usable trunk space—but not until later in the '92 model run. "Purple Haze" metallic was a new body color this year, reflecting GM's return to some shades that might suggest the long-gone muscle-car era, which happened to coincide with the colorful counterculture period of the late Sixties and early Seventies.

Fuel mileage was passable but still no bargain in these final seasons of the third generation. A V-6-equipped RS convertible with five-speed tested by CONSUMER GUIDE® averaged 17.8 mpg, while a Z28 with the 5.7-liter V-8 got 15.8 mpg. Hardly frugal, but it could have been worse—and had been, just a few short years earlier. On the other hand, all engines ran on regular-

The '91 Z28 (*this page and red cars, opposite*) could be had with the 170/205/230-horsepower 5.0-liter V-8 or the Corvette-derived 5.7-liter, with 245 horses. Retail price for the hatchback version was $15,445 and a healthy $20,815 for the ragtop Z28. Most buff-book writers praised the '91 Z for its aggressive acceleration and exceptional handling, but were put off by the car's lack of anti-lock braking. The black-and-white RS (*opposite, bottom*) was a Special Service Package for police departments.

octane gasoline, while quite a few competitors demanded premium.

Police fleets could order a Special Service Package (RPO B4C) for the RS that included either the 5.0- or 5.7-liter V-8, dual performance exhaust, a performance suspension, P245/50ZR16 tires, all-disc brakes, limited-slip rear axle, engine oil cooler, 150-amp alternator, and air conditioning. The smaller V-8 came with a five-speed transmission; the 5.7-liter with 4-speed automatic.

(continued on page 122)

The Heritage Appearance option package was available for $175 on all '92 Camaros, to mark a real milestone: Camaro's 25th anniversary. Package buyers could choose Arctic White, Bright Red, or Black. Wide stripes over hood and trunklid were the most obvious visual cues, as seen on the Z28 (*this page*) and the RS convertible (*opposite*). Heritage Appearance notwithstanding, all '92 Camaros received a commemorative dash emblem.

By 1992, Camaros had been sold and driven in four different decades—an impressive achievement. As the car's handsome third generation wound down, it did so with the familiar flair intact. Other cars were more sophisticated, more modern, but none had Camaro's unique personality. Whether opting for a '92 RS coupe (*top*) or Z28 convertible (*above*), buyers could be confident that they were participating in one of Detroit's most enduring success stories.

"Camaro owners have a special relationship with their cars," Chevrolet explained, "and many drivers consider the car an extension of themselves." For years, its allure had struck in several ways. "The RS is especially appealing to single women who appreciate the Camaro's sporty styling and fun-to-drive quotient, while the Z28 attracts single males who like the car's

athletic looks, ride and handling." While an automaker's evaluation of the appeal of one of its own cars isn't always 100 percent reliable, Chevy's explanation hits close to the mark. In the next chapter, we'll look at some of the qualities that keep this old relic in demand, and at the exciting new fourth-generation design that will propel Camaro into the future.

Chapter Eleven

Wild Things: Camaro Hangs On

Now in its exciting fourth generation, Camaro continues to dazzle its fans with ponycar allure. Undeniably, Camaro has its share of quirks—failings, some may say. Yet the car has endured by offering style, performance, and, especially, a vibrant personality.

Camaro fans were heartened by the news that their favorite ponycar (along with its Firebird counterpart), would be back for 1993—and with a sleek new fourth-generation design, at that. Continuing as a rear-drive, 4-seat, 3-door hatchback coupe, the '93 Camaro hit showrooms in January of that year. The base model dropped its RS tag, but the high-performance variant again wore the Z28 badge. Alas, a convertible was not immediately available, and wasn't scheduled to return until after the '93 model year.

Styling was more modern than before yet clearly in the familiar Camaro idiom. The dent-resistant fiberglass-like composite material that was used on the '92's ground effects trim and front and rear fascias was used for the '93's front fenders, doors, roof, and rear hatch. Curb weight rose by about 150 pounds, to 3241 for the base model and 3396 for the Z28.

Engine choices were pared from four to two. 1992's 3.1-liter V-6 was enlarged to 3.4 liters, with horsepower increasing from 140 to 160; torque came in at 200 pounds-feet at 3600 rpm. The 3.4 was standard on the base Camaro. Both the 5.0-liter V-8 and previous 5.7-liter V-8 were dropped; the '93 Z28 came standard with a new 5.7 V-8, the same LT1 engine introduced for '92 on the Corvette. In Camaro guise, the engine cranked out 275 horsepower, 25 fewer than in the 'Vette; torque was a robust 325 pounds-feet at 2000 rpm.

A 5-speed manual transmission was standard with the V-6, and a new, American-made Borg Warner 6-speed manual came standard with the Z28. Optional for both '93s was a 4-speed overdrive automatic. Z28 buyers could buy extra oomph with an optional 3.23 performance axle ratio in place of the standard 2.73.

Base Camaros came standard with front-disc/rear-drum brakes; the Z28 with front and rear discs. Anti-lock brakes were newly optional on both, though the base-model ABS setup retained rear drums. A passenger-side air bag joined the driver-side air bag that was carried over from the '92.

A removable T-top could be ordered with either model; other optional goodies included a compact disc player, 6-way power driver's seat, power windows/ mirrors/locks/hatch release, and a rear defogger.

Camaro's fourth generation is unarguably more sophisticated than the ones that preceded it, yet picky types will nevertheless be compelled to ask: Isn't it outmoded? In basic structure, perhaps, but each year's version adopts a few more modern-day electronic marvels, to force performance and efficiency ever higher—but without losing the car's basic nature. Granted, a spin in a Camaro reminds some people of a jarring trek in a tightly sprung truck, especially if the road is less than sea-smooth. Like most rear-drive automobiles,

Camaros can be treacherous on icy roads, demanding even more concentration than usual. For Camaro's admirers, on the other hand, each tour brings back memories of one's first car; or that extra-special automobile you owned all those years ago, be it a Studebaker Hawk, a Ford Mustang, or an earlier-generation Camaro.

A Camaro demands attention from its driver—and tolerance from its passenger. All the more so when it carries a manual gearbox. A modern compact's shifter tends to be cordial and forgiving, practically saying to the clumsy operator who's made it hurt on the way from second to third gear: "That's okay. I forgive you. Let's just try that again."

Grab a Camaro's billiard-ball gearshift knob and it's another story when you make a mistake slamming from one ratio to the next. "Hey you!" the angry transmission and clutch almost seem to cry, "Watch it! If you can't do it right, get out of there and leave me alone!" And when you grasp that knob, you actually feel the car's vibrations, as though it were alive, not detached and aloof as in most modern-day automobiles.

Just listen to those throbbing exhaust pipes, that fast-idling engine, the pulse-raising sounds that you feel as well as hear. Watch the tach needle shoot up as you tap the gas. Revel in the slippery motion of that slick gearbox—the kind that all cars should have, but don't. Shift it gently, or slam it hard—Camaro doesn't care. Feel the sure-footed confidence in the steering

wheel, the firm support of its seat, in a cockpit created with drivers in mind. Experience the sticky grip of the tires as you round a demanding curve, thrill to the car's raw energy as the curve evolves into a straight line—then brace yourself as a pothole approaches.

Then get ready to drag out a thick billfold when it's time to gas up. A Nineties Camaro is not exactly economical, at least around town (though it's far more frugal than its ancestors). EPA mileage ratings are comparable to today's full-size sedans: perhaps 17-19 mpg in the city, but as good as 28 mpg on the open road. (To eke out figures like that, of course, you'll have to keep a feathery foot on the gas pedal.)

Even for the conservation-minded among us, a trial run with a Camaro can evoke irresistible temptation—a guilty pleasure that arises as you feel the heart thumping and the blood racing.

In this day of twin-cam sixes and front-drive layouts, engineering sophisticates might snort at the appeal of an old-fashioned, rear-wheel-drive coupe and a muscular V-8 engine. Let them. Camaro fans ignore the barbs, and enjoy their own distinct measure of pleasure, whether on the road or at the track. They're people who crave a little rowdiness in their motoring lives, and who are willing to endure a discomfort or two to get it.

Even a seemingly tame modern-day Camaro with a V-6 emits hearty, thorough-bred sounds from the engine and a subtly burbling growl from its twin tailpipes, which mask the lack of serious muscularity underhood. Then again, tromping the gas of a V-6 Camaro with manual shift delivers a startling snap into action, helped by the coupe's low standard first-gear ratio. One could easily imagine that a V-8 was providing the fun.

Camaro fans are a bit like the folks who braved chill winds and leaky roofs for the excitement of driving a British roadster in the 1950s. Motoring wasn't simply a matter of moving from point A to point B in blissful comfort; no, it was an *experience.* Those nonconformists wanted a car they could drive, not simply point; a car with character, one that seemed almost to look down its nose at the humdrum "modern" rivals encountered along life's superhighways.

To put it simply, Camaros of *any* vintage, yesterday's or today's, deliver a blast of sensations right out of the past. Untamed, unbridled, unforgiving. While at the wheel

General Motors' startling decision to dramatically streamline operations threw a scare into everyone who loves the Camaro. Happily, GM brought Chevy's ponycar (and its Firebird cousin) back for a swoopy fourth generation (*this page and opposite*). Camaro engine choices for 1993 were a 3.4-liter V-6 rated at 160 horsepower, and a new, Corvette-based 5.7-liter V-8 that cranked out 275 horses; the latter engine came standard with the hot Z28 (*above*). The convertible seen opposite, below, is a heavily disguised styling proposal; the real fourth-generation ragtop would not be available until after the '93 model year.

of a hot Camaro (or even a mild Camaro), you're prepared for stimulation, virtually girded for battle—even when engaged in nothing more thrilling than commuting to work.

Some call the Camaro a car for kids—or even a tool for masochists. Maybe so, but it tends to bring out the kid in most of us. Then too, the folks who scoff are the ones least likely to buy a car of this nature—or, for that matter, to be reading these words. For them, the showrooms are full of sophisticated front-drivers. Camaro's legions of avid followers, who value passion above practicality, can only hope that Chevrolet will not drop its "wild things" in the foreseeable future, or transform them beyond easy recognition.

Index